Road To Top Flight

Guide To Restoration Planning

First Edition

by Paul Iaffaldano

Published by Horsepower Publishing
P.O. Box 391
Palatine, IL 60078-0391

U.S.A. $17.95

Published by Horsepower Publishing
P.O. Box 391, Palatine, Illinois 60078-0391

Photography by - Paul Iaffaldano, Gary Mueller, Eric Bethel
Literary Editor - Talie McKenzie

Printed in the United States of America

Library of Congress Cataloging-in-Publication Data
Iaffaldano, Paul, 1956-
Road To Top Flight / Paul Iaffaldano. -- first edition
Library of Congress Catalog Card Number: 94-96765
ISBN 1-886542-00-7

This book is designed to help you plan a restoration project on any vintage or classic car. I have used the restoration of a 1959 Corvette to illustrate how the important choices were made before and during an actual restoration process. I strongly encourage you - no I challenge you - to read this book and deliberate, as I did, the tough decisions that must be made to create a show winner from an undriveable wreck.

The Road Map

This book is dedicated to three hot little Corvettes:
Patricia, Paige, and Blair

Restoring a car can be equal parts challenge and reward. Though never simple, careful forethought can help you avoid obstacles and see the project through to its completion.

A poorly planned, improperly executed restoration, on the other hand, can be something more akin to your worst nightmare. Problems will arise. Parts won't be correct. And you'll quickly lose interest and money as the project drags on for months and months.

Forward

This book goes a long way towards helping you avoid the pitfalls and realize your restoration goals. Paul Iaffaldano has gone down the often bumpy restoration road with his 1959 Corvette; he's hit a few pot-holes along the way but remained true to his course and ultimately reached his destination unscathed and with a beautiful car to show for it. They are his experiences that you will find in the next hundred pages; his triumphs and his failures. And every page can teach you something about the restoration process.

Still it is important to point out that this book alone will not ensure your restoration efforts will end in success. For that, you will need to amass vast knowledge of the particular make, model and year vehicle you will restore, learning the correct finish and placement of every nut, bolt and wire-tie from bumper to bumper, tires to roof. And you'll need the determination and will to see the project through - two things no how-to book can provide for you.

I'm often reminded that with restorations, as with most other things in life, the journey is the reward. Restoring your favorite car will not only leave you with a vehicle others will be envious of, but it will also leave you with a deeper understanding of yourself, and a pride that relatively few people can truly understand.

With that, I will wish you well on your adventures that lie ahead, and will look forward to meeting you on the show fields someday to admire your accomplishments and hear of your journey.

Jason Scott

"Begin with the End"

Chapter 1 — Goals

My goal was clear, concise, and straightforward. Or so I thought. I wanted to restore my 1959 Corvette to top award winning standards.

What I had not counted on was my own urge to create something more than correct. I wanted to create something perfect; something that reflected the original beauty and grace of a Corvette, without some of its more prominent assembly line birthmarks.

It looks close to impossible, but this undrivable wreck will be step-by-step restored to within 95% of original condition as defined by NCRS. This will be no easy feat for a car that is 35 years old.

An award winning show car can mean many different things, ranging from custom creations that express an owner's personalized interpretations to scrupulously accurate representations of historically correct automobiles. I love both. But the historically correct interpretation represents a particularly interesting challenge that requires knowledge from research and understanding as well as the craftsmanship and creativity of a custom project. The route I chose to follow - recreating an historically accurate car - was a personal choice. I certainly respect the decisions of those who choose differently.

"recreating an historically accurate car"

My selection of an early Corvette was not by accident. True, I am a sports car enthusiast and have been a Corvette fan almost from birth. But, the Corvette is a good example for this book because of the strength of the organized support groups for Corvette afficionados that provide extremely detailed and well documented research and literature.

Therefore, restoring an early Corvette would provide the type of challenge that could be easily transferred to the restoration of other cars that do not have an abundance of historical written data. The issues and steps would be the same. In fact, cars with fewer organized clubs tend to have less stringent judging criteria making the end product slightly easier to accomplish.

The National Corvette Restorers Society (NCRS) has published some very thick manuals that describe "correctness". NCRS guidelines are indisputably the most complete within Corvette circles as well as the best documented source for understanding historical correctness of early Corvettes. An enormous amount of research has been compiled by individuals who have years of experience designing, building, and repairing Corvettes. Often the information comes from actual Chevrolet technical or production files that have been verified and refined through numerous surveys of Corvette owners.

Twenty years old, the NCRS has more than 12,560 members, making it the largest Corvette organization in the country. The NCRS Judging Manual is used by every major Corvette enthusiast to evaluate cars.

Using NCRS data on production numbers, it seems that Corvette J59S108027 was built on or around June 3, 1959. This date can be calculated by extrapolating from the end of the month production figures. For example, the last car built on May 29, 1959, was car #7934 while the last car built on June 30, 1959 was #8702. Therefore, 768 cars were produced in June during 22 production days - or roughly 34.9 cars per day. My car, #8027, was the 93rd car of the month, which would mean it was probably born some time in the afternoon of the third day of production or June 3, 1959.

My goal was to restore my 1959 Corvette VIN #J59S108027 from "undrivable" to NCRS Top-Flight standards. Those standards reflect an "as it came off the factory line and after standard/typical dealer preparation" philosophy. Those standards go a long way to helping everyone preserve cars in an historically correct manner. They also serve as a valuable tool to evaluate exactly what is original and what is not.

The VIN was also stamped on the frame of the car, but it is only visible once the body has been lifted from the frame. Incidentally, about 10% of early Corvettes had the VIN stamped twice on the frame as #8027 did.

My preference was to take a few minor detours from the "factory line/dealer prep" point of view to a restoration that would reflect a "how it was intended to be" philosophy. For example, Harley Earl, head of General Motors Styling and Design, and Zora Arkus-Dontov, Chief Corvette Engineer, did not intend for the intake manifolds to receive overspray. That they did was a function of production sloppiness. In summary, I will not replicate all of the "mistakes or blemishes" that were introduced on the assembly line. I will not change the character of the car. Nor will I stretch the "intended to be" interpretation beyond what could reasonably be expected or hoped for during the period in which the car was built. Suspension parts that were painted black during production will be painted black on my restored car. Simply put, I am willing to sacrifice a few NCRS judging points to make the car more to my liking. I encourage anyone to do the same as long as the decision is informed, not something done out of ignorance.

The first step towards buying or restoring any Corvette should be the purchase of a $30 NCRS Judging Manual for the specific year or class car in which you are interested. The NCRS Judging Manual will explain exactly how a Corvette should appear to be considered original (or at least correct). In most cases, any Corvette novice with a little car knowledge can determine if parts are correct or not.

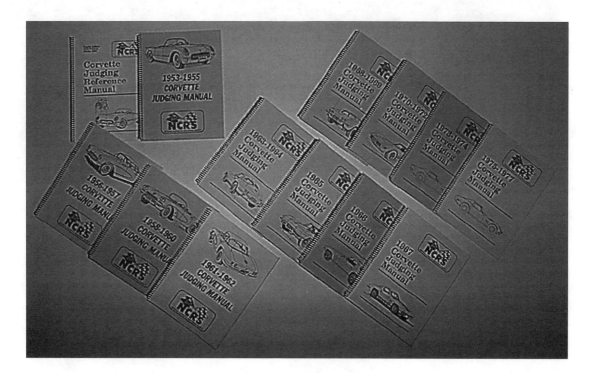

The finished car will reflect the grace and beauty of the car as its designers intended it to be.

"Begin with the End"

The sum total of this book will give you a good feel for "what needs to be done" to bring a car to Top Flight condition.

Along our "Road to Top Flight", our drive will take us through the following twelve topics. I hope you'll join us.

1.   Begin with the End - Before starting the restoration process, understand why you want to restore a car. You will be surprised how it impacts your decisions.

2.   Planning - How do you find professional help? How do you find the right car?

3.   Simple Patience - Many options exist for body repair. Several criteria will dictate which is the right one for you.

4.   Degree of Correctness - What kind of paint? What color? How should it be applied? Each decision will have an impact on whether you achieve your goals.

5.   Beauty of the Beast - More than a little preparation work is necessary. Watch out for short cuts that can leave your paint looking bad.

6.   Blasting Black - It is easy to restore a frame, but it is also vital that it be right.

7.   Heart of the Machine - having the correct components can mean the difference between a valuable classic and "replicar" status.

8.   Performance Original - Which is preferable: Rebuilding to original performance or exceeding it?

9.   Importance of Being Detailed - The quality of a restoration is often determined in the final weeks of reassembling all the parts. Do you know what to look for?

10. Why are We Here? - What are you really after? An expert gives some clues.

11. Enjoy Your Car. Isn't that why you started this anyway?

12. Worksheets - These sheets are designed to help you plan a successful project.

"Planning"

Chapter 2 — Who and What

Some people like to drive down a road by themselves. The decisions they make are all their own. The same dynamics apply when restoring a car. Those who travel alone become intimately familiar with every part of their cars. But, just as a navigator can help plan a correct course on a road trip, so a professional restorer with vast experience can help steer you around many costly and time consuming mistakes.

I chose to travel "The Road to Top-Flight" with a guide, someone with Corvette wisdom and broad knowledge of the car's rich history. Making that decision was easy for me. I already had a full-time job and am married with two young children. I knew that I didn't have the hours and hours of time needed to properly restore a car. A professional, especially one with lots of specific Corvette experience and correct tools at his finger tips, will spend 1,000 hours of labor restoring a car. I am told an enthusiastic amateur will spend two to three times that amount of time for a full frame-off..

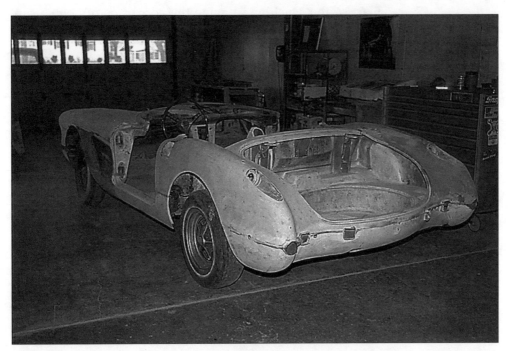

The average restoration requires more than 1,000 hours of labor and more than $17,000 in parts. Even if the car had driven well, most of the components would have had to be totally restored, so the hours and cost would not deviate much from the average.

In addition to the time savings, I believed that using a professional would save on parts costs. I had estimated that parts alone for this project would cost more than $17,000. Actual costs were more like $21,000. The project would have been considerably more expensive if I had purchased incorrect or unnecessary parts. A professional is also in a better position to negotiate prices on used parts.

Professionals can also help avoid mistakes in the tiny detail areas that are so important to top flighting a car. For example, many suppliers sell parts that they claim are correct but which actually will not meet judging standards. I did not feel qualified as a novice to handle this part of the project without help. If your expertise is different, you may make a different decision.

I believed my time was better spent finding the right professional for the job. I sought one who would fit my needs and be experienced at restoring cars to top flight condition.

All things considered, I opted for a small but experienced category of restorers. Incidentally, this category is probably the most difficult to find. They aren't large enough to advertise extensively, and they may not be in your backyard. (See the Focus Box for tips on which kind of restoration expertise is right for you.)

I traveled extensively within a seven state area to find a restoration expert who had what I was looking for: someone with the professional qualifications I sought as well as someone I liked personally.

Any potential risk of picking a smaller restoration shop was carefully minimized since I reviewed his work very carefully and talked to several owners of cars that he had restored. When I scrupulously examined his shop, I found it to have all the tools and equipment I was looking for. Also, his shop is extremely well organized. (I believe you have a much higher chance of getting good work from someone with a clean, well organized shop.)

My candidate was one of many with experience, references, skills, and resources. Beyond looking at these attributes, I picked someone who seemed to be honest. He is honest enough to give an opinion when asked; honest enough to be realistic about deadlines.

Type of Restorer

The following chart lists the three types of professional restorers and the major advantages and disadvantages of each type:

1. Local mechanic:

Defining Characteristics:

- Does mostly mechanical work
- Works on mostly late model cars
- Does not have, or has limited show car experience

Major Advantages:

- Local nature makes it easy to monitor progress
- Potentially least expensive option
- Might be great source for well defined restoration projects

Major Disadvantages:

- Could be very difficult to achieve top award quality
- May not be able to plan and execute full restoration

2. Small but experienced restoration shop:

Defining Characteristics:

- Restores fewer than five complete cars per year
- Has extensive experience with older cars including your specific model
- Has restored cars to top award condition

Major Advantages:

- Your car receives much personal attention from the expert (less hired help)
- Mid-priced option
- Able to plan and execute full restoration project

Major Disadvantages:

- Small shop nature usually means longer restoration times
- Lack of national reputation could mean more risky option

3. Large well-known restoration shop:

Defining Characteristics:

- Restores more than 10 complete cars per year
- Is well known nationally within club circles
- Has restored special cars with national recognition

Major Advantages:

- Absolutely the safest, best way to get a top award restoration
- Usually best at meeting deadlines

Major Disadvantages:

- Very, very expensive
- May have to travel longer distances making progress harder to monitor

Before you turn the page, please note:

Next to finding the best resources for the technical restoration, selecting the right car to restore is the most important decision. If you can, try to avoid buying a car before you have identified help. Your restoration expert can help you evaluate cars so you will not buy a car that will exceed your restoration budget.

The following section outlines how we evaluated our project car. A work sheet is included in the last chapter that will help you evaluate cars you are considering.

selecting the right car to restore

The Frame:

WHAT TO LOOK FOR:	HOW #8027 FARED:
1. Look closely to see the extent of rust. All frames have some rust (the key is to make sure the rust is not too deep. The rear cross member usually shows the most rust).	*Not badly rusted car from Texas.*
2. A badly rusted frame will weaken the car's foundation making the body shift over time.	*Outstanding that the rear cross bar did not have any pitting at all.*
3. Repairing a frame is one of the most costly and difficult repairs to make to a Corvette.	*Frame grade:* **A+**

Although the VIN #8027 frame has a lot of surface rust, it has absolutely no pitting nor deterioration, even at the rear crossmember.

selecting the right car to restore

The Body:

WHAT TO LOOK FOR:	HOW #8027 FARED:
1. Assess damage. Some fiberglass damage is easy and less costly to fix, while other damage is very expensive.	*The cowl area is in good shape; no major damage.*
2. The cowl area and passenger compartment is most important as it is the core of the car and very complicated to fix.	*The front nose and front driver fender are damaged. Also, the rear fender is cracked.*
3. Damage to the nose area or fenders is easier to fix.(watch out for damage to rear fenders. Replacement parts will not meet original factory specifications.)	***Body grade: C+***

With damage to the nose, front left fender and rear right fender, the body work can be repaired without a trace through patient and knowledgeable efforts. The key is to make repairs at the factory seams using factory-style bonding strips.

selecting the right car to restore

Drive Train:

WHAT TO LOOK FOR:

1. If you can find a car with its original motor, transmission, and rearend, you will save money and time trying to track down current replacements.

2. With early cars, it is very difficult to know if engines are original. You can tell if they are correct.

3. Don't worry about condition because you will have the drive train rebuilt as part of the restoration.

HOW #8027 FARED:

Strongly suspect that the transmission and rear end are original.

The motor is correct, but it is probably not original.

Drive train grade: B

The 4 speed Borg Warner transmission and the rear end are very probably original. The build date on the main transmission is February 1959, four months prior to the car's assembly date. The tail housing was cast June 29, 1958, a full eleven months prior to the car's build date. This can be typical of parts that did not change over several years.

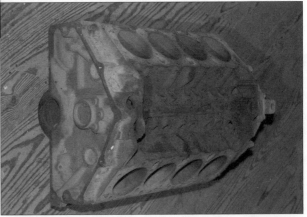

The engine is probably not original, but it is the correct casting number, casting date, and build date/stamping for this car.

selecting the right car to restore
Replacement Parts:

WHAT TO LOOK FOR:	HOW #8027 FARED:
1. Stainless window windshield frames	*Very Nice*
2. Dash/Instrument panel	*Good but no tach*
3. Bumper (very expensive to replace)	*Very Nice*
4. Glass (expensive to find correctly dated)	*None!*
5. Radio (more than $500 for Wonderbar)	*None!!*
Total Difficult Parts	**Grade: C**
Convertible Top, Brakes, Vinyl Interiors, Tires, Radiator	
Total Easy Parts	**Grade: D-**

Total Evaluation for 1959 Corvette VIN #8027:

This is a good candidate for restoration. It will not be the easiest project, but it is restorable.

Overall Grade: B-

The firewall, cowl, and passenger area are very difficult to repair correctly. They are in good condition on VIN #8027.

"Simple Patience"

Chapter 3 — Body Repair

This is the most important chapter you will read if you are considering restoring or buying a restored Classic Car. The body is the largest and most visible part of the car. Although the fiberglass body is the most unique part of a Corvette and restoring fiberglass is completely different than restoring metal, the principle strategy used is very similar to that used on metal cars.

The expert we consulted has learned his art over years of trial and error and is not so keen on sharing his secrets. It sounds like a cliché, but body work is an art. However, in this chapter you will find some valuable tips that you cannot find at your local repair shop.

During the first part of our journey I will focus on fiberglass repairs that even the most perfect "no-hit" bodies will need. These include repairs to stress cracks and in the case of my car some significant

It may look impossible, but this 1959 Corvette will be totally restored to Top-Flight standards. It is quite evident we had much work ahead of us to bring this body up to original, factory specifications. We repaired some body panels, but most of the damage was replaced with new fiberglass body panels that are exactly as they came from the factory.

damage to various body panels. Some of the damage had already been repaired by previous owners. All of those repairs will probably have to be completely redone to bring them up to NCRS standards of originality.

Before I start describing repairs, I will give you a basic understanding of how Corvettes were put together. First, each individual body part was made of press molded fiberglass, fiberglass that was pressed between two molds, one for the inside and one for the outside of the part. The result is a part that is smooth on both sides. Also 80% of the resin is forced out of the panel when it is pressed making the part more flexible and less susceptible to shrinking and warping.

Many suppliers have parts in their catalog that are not press molded. These parts are simply not acceptable to NCRS standards. They are not like the factory assembly line parts and definitely not what the car's designers intended.

The second element that is important to know is how the body parts were joined together. Corvettes were not one giant piece of fiberglass, but several pieces or panels carefully joined together. Actually, one of the challenges of early Corvette development was the technology of joining these sections together. Chevrolet's solution was to use bonding strips as a stabilizing element in joining two pieces of fiberglass together. The bonding strips served two purposes: they provided a way to line up the panels to form a smooth even exterior surface; they provided a needed element of structural support at what might otherwise to a weak spot.

A Corvette body is actually made from several smaller body panels. The dotted lines on this crude illustration show the separations between the various body panels.

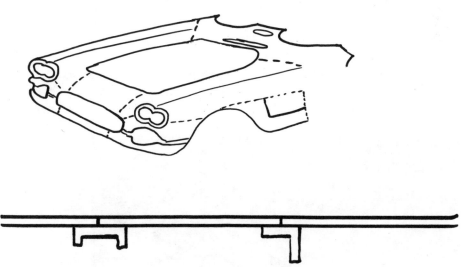

This simple drawing shows a cross section of how a bonding strip is used to join and reinforce two panels. Note how it would serve to align the exterior surface, and the perpendicular element would add structural rigidity. The example on the left is used in most of the side body joints. The example on the right is used in the front nose joints.

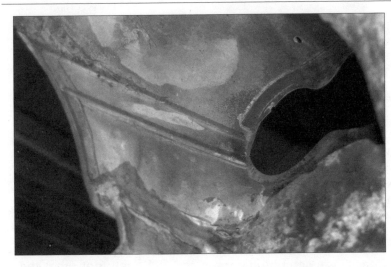

From the inside of the wheel well, this bonding strip joined the upper fender with the lower front nose section. Note how the strip of fiberglass is bent at the edge to give it even more structural rigidity.

As we pointed out in the first chapter, the body on Corvette VIN #8027 had quite a bit of damage. The cowl/firewall area was intact so my repairs would not require a total rebuild. However, my car had five areas that would need professional attention:

- the upper and lower front panels
- the driver's side lower front corner
- the driver's side front fender from the cove down
- the passenger side rear quarter panel
- the hood

Repair Routes

The first step was to strip the old paint off the car. We used the old fashioned method of brushing on paint stripper and scraping off the bubbly mess. The stripper took the top layers of paint off the car but did not remove the primer coat. The primer needs to be removed by sanding. We then sanded through to the bare fiberglass, which allowed a clean look at exactly what the damage was to each element needing repair. In my case, the initial assessment was correct. We found no surprises.

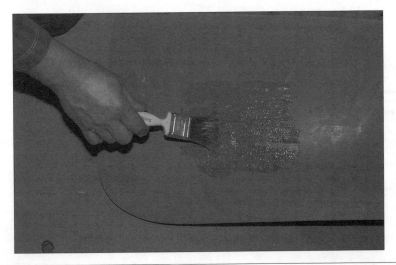

Removing the top coats of paint is best done by brushing paint remover on one section of the car at a time. The remover will penetrate all the way down to the primer, but not remove the primer.

When the liquid remover starts to bubble, scrape all the paint off the car using a plastic scraper.

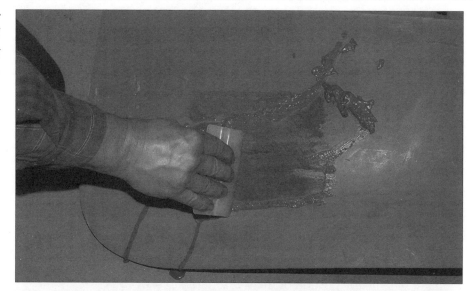

The primer must be sanded off. It is best to use a fine grit #200 paper with an orbital sander. The orbital motion will help reduce the sanding marks in the fiberglass.

The fiberglass should have a light tan or yellowish cast. The bare fiberglass will allow you to fully access the required body repairs. In our case, no surprises were found in the extent of fiberglass damage.

Three methods can be used to repair broken fiberglass: repair; replace with a new part; replace with an original part. We used all three methods on my car, picking the option that would successfully duplicate original factory standards for each problem area to be repaired.

I have three cautions relating to this stage in the restoration process:

1. It is imperative that the end result of fiberglass repair be a smooth outer body shell.Keep this in mind when joining body panels together and setting door and hood gaps.

2. The bonding strips and joints should be located where they were originally on the car.

3. The inside portion of the workmanship should be somewhat sloppy. The assembly line workers were only concerned with the outside appearance which usually resulted in adhesive oozing from elements like bonding strips.

Achieving the best overall fit of the various body panels, like doors, requires an extra step that in the long run will save time and result in a better finished product. The extra step involves removing the body from the frame and installing a new body mount kit including mounting shims before you have done any repair work. Drop the body back on the frame with the new mounting kit in place. This trick will let you add or sand off fiberglass, set door gaps, and straighten the overall body with the confidence of knowing that the parts will fit the same way once you have redone the rest of the car.

Take the body back off the frame later, carefully marking the position of all of the mounting parts.

Damage Repair

The next series of photos give you an overview of how to repair a minor crack and how to replace a body panel.

When the damage is not at a stress point and the fiberglass the crack is not damaged, then a good option to consider is repairing the existing body panel. The following series of pictures outlines the process for repairing the damage.

This is a pretty large crack in the fiberglass. However, the damage does not extend beyond the area that is visually cracked. Also, this panel is not under significant stress and, therefore, is unlikely to re-crack or re-fracture in the future.

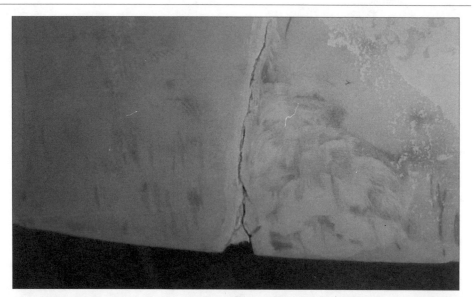

The first step is to grind out all the loose or damaged fiberglass in the area of the crack. A small, high speed tool works well for this.

When all the loose stuff is removed, the crack will appear larger, but the repair material will have solid undamaged fiberglass to grab onto.

Cut a strip of fiberglass to use as a bonding piece on the under side of the body panel. Unlike the bonding strips that are used to join two body panels together, this strip should be flat and not have its edges bend parallel for structural support. You will want to hide this strip as it is not considered original factory production.

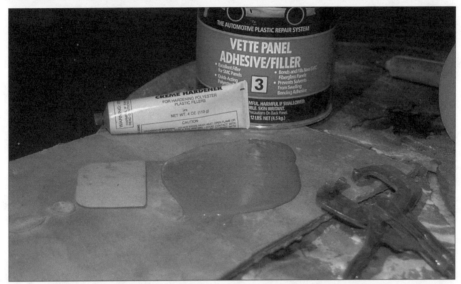

The crack will be filled with a two part Vette Bond product. This adhesive will also bond the strip to the body panel.

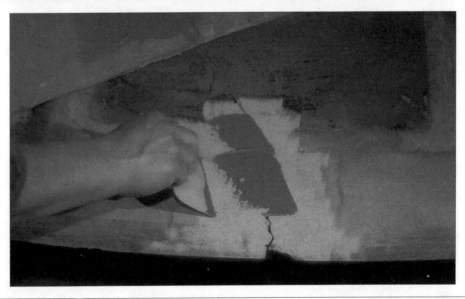

Spread the Vette Bond on the back of the strip and force it into the fiberglass crack. Place the bonding strip on the inside of the body panel.

Clamp the bonding strip in place allowing room to work around the clamps. Spread more Vette Bond on the strip in a way that leaves a smooth surface that conceals the bonding strip.

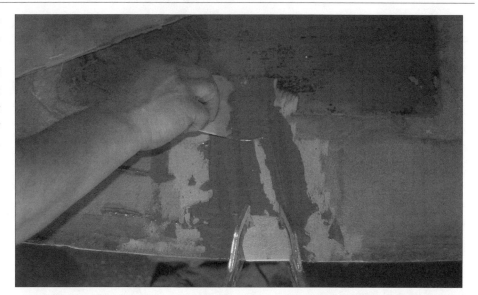

On the outside of the panel, make sure the crack is completely filled in with Vette Bond. In fact, it is a good idea to build up the thickness of the repair.

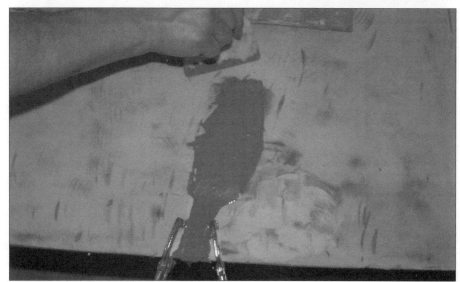

Let the Vette Bond set up. Do not let it dry overnight, because it will be too hard to work with. The small grinding wheel works well for removing the excess material. There should be no lumps or projections when the grinding is complete.

Now that the structural part of the repair is complete, apply body filler to fill any tiny air holes or imperfections in the surface.

When the body filler has dried to the consistency of fudge, use an orbital sanding pad to further shape the filler to the body contours.

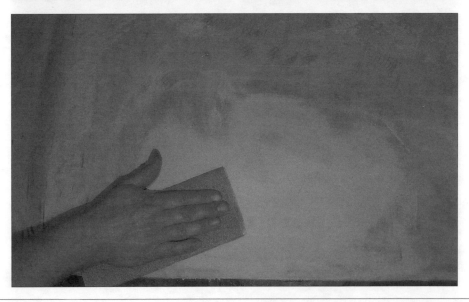

After the body filler has fully dried, but not overnight, finish the sanding with fine #100 to #200 grade sandpaper.

Replace Entire Panels

When the damage is extensive or involves areas of the car that provide structural support, the damaged areas should be replaced. For almost all front end and other commonly damaged areas, press molded replacement parts are available. Areas like the rear quarter panels are rarely damaged. Even through professional contacts, we could not find a supplier of press molded rear quarter panels. I opted to take the needed part from a wrecked car of the same year.

New or original, both are identical for Top-Flight standards. The repair process is the same and is outlined in the photos below.

Both the front left cove and the right rear quarter have fiberglass damage that requires the body panels to be replaced. The cove can be replaced with a new press molded piece. The rear quarter will be replaced with one from a parts car.

The old damaged fiber-glass panel needs to be cut from the car. It is extremely important that the cuts are made along the panel seams. The replacement parts will fit easily, and, more importantly, the bonding strips will be replaced in their proper place on the inside of the car body.

"Degree of Correctness"

Chapter 4 — Paint Type

Since the beginning of the restoration process, I have anxiously awaited the day my car would be painted. Everyone has his own private reasons for loving cars. My passion has a lot to do with a belief that cars are modern art. Nothing in the restoration process will contribute more to the style and beauty of this 1959 Corvette than the choice of paint.

> Everyone has his own private reasons for loving cars.

It seems that "original looking paint" can have several interpretations. To help you form your own opinion, this chapter outlines various options.

For me, the painting process was successful. The car's new paint looks as it probably did when it rolled off the assembly line. As with all of the restoration processes, my goal was to make the paint exterior look as it originally was intended.

Within NCRS circles some controversy exists about the interpretation of this guideline. Is the intent to look like original paint or to actually be original paint? The NCRS Judging Standard says, "Cars are to be judged to the standard of vehicle appearance, and as equipped, at the time and point of final assembly by the Chevrolet Motor Division of General Motors Corporation. Presentation for judging is to be in the condition normally associated with that of a Corvette which has undergone the then-current standard Chevrolet Dealer New Car Preparation for delivery to a purchaser, exclusive of any dealer or purchaser inspired additions, deletions or changes."

What is the correct paint?

Some NCRS members have a more rigid interpretation of this point than other members. The question revolves around the type of paint to use. Simply put, is lacquer or a lacquer look-alike preferred?

Corvettes were painted in lacquer until fairly recently. One property of the paint is that it has a deep glow. Another property of lacquer is that it never really completely dries. It emits vapor from the thinner used in the application process several years after the paint has been applied.

The real problem is the way in which it is applied to a car. In many states, using lacquer paint is illegal. It is extremely toxic and has many detrimental effects on the environment, including releasing gases that destroy the ozone layer. In 1994, it does not seem ethical to use a product so selfishly when environmentally safe substitutes are available. Within a few years lacquer will probably be illegal everywhere.

Fortunately, NCRS has a reasonable view on this. While the club will not come straight out and say not using lacquer is acceptable, the guidelines are written in a manner that allows a restorer the flexibility to do what he/she thinks is correct environmentally as well as for the car. Originality is scored on appearance according to section 3, paragraph 9 of the Judging Manual. "A successful judging, such as body paint, does not mean the existing paint is that which was originally applied at the factory, but does imply it appears as though it could be." The word "appears" is key.

The goal of the painting process is to make the paint appear as it did 35 years ago. A polyurethane paint applied to look like lacquer was my solution. I did not use any coating or clear finishing products. The finished paint was wet sanded and buffed to remove the orange peel (bumps).

A letter from Dennis Clark, National Judging Chairman for NCRS, was published in the Spring 1994 issue of *The Corvette Restorer* that addresses the question clearly. "The obvious use of any coating system such as enamel, polyurethane, or clear lacquer shall receive a total deduction on originality points." He further discusses that obvious may be subjective including how many points should be deducted for incorrect paint.

I have also kept true to my own goal: to make this car as it was intended to be by its designers removing only its more obvious assembly line birth defects. I would not go beyond what the car's designers intended. The fact that clear was not applied in the production process is not due to production sloppiness; clear was not available to Chevrolet production at that time.

I drew the line at not making the paint look better than it possibly could have in 1959. I did not want the paint to have a glossier finish. This would have taken the restoration a step beyond original. Since I would store VIN #8027 in a garage and under a cover, I felt the need for protective clear was minimal.

As a last thought on this subject. It is your decision. You should make your own statement regardless of losing a few points at a car show. You may want to be totally precise and use lacquer. You may want to make your car look its best and use clear. My only advice would be that you make an informed decision.

This 1959 Corvette is painted its original Roman Red color after months of hard preparation work. The body is on a special jig that allows it to be rotated for more even painting.

Having the body on a hoist makes buffing the hard-to-reach places a lot easier on the back. It will also be helpful for applying the under coating.

My first choices for new colors for VIN #8027 were horizon blue with ermine white coves. This metallic color looks exceedingly sophisticated. The early cars did not have paint codes on the VIN tags, so a car receiving a full frame off and a thorough paint job can be painted any color the owner chooses.

What color?

However, during the restoration process a few ways to verify the car's original color can be tried. The paint color was written in crayon on the trunk wall and could be revealed after the cardboard backing was removed and any overspray was stripped away.

The second way was to look for overspray in the passenger area once the seats and carpet were removed. The inside of the glove box and other parts that are unlikely to be repainted can also yield color clues.

The color of the car was marked in grease crayon on the trunk wall. The marking is on the bare fiberglass that will be visible when the paint and primer are removed from the back of the trunk.

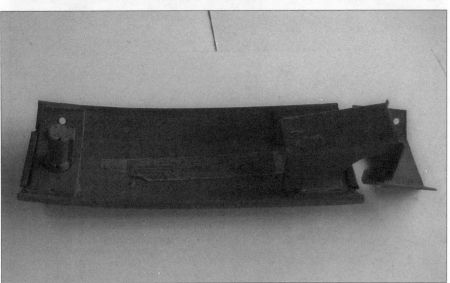

Another sign that the car was originally Roman Red was the inside of the glove box. The original fuel warning notice was still on the glove box door. It is highly unlikely that a new sticker would have been applied if the car had been repainted.

After checking all of these areas, I was 99.9% sure that the car was originally Roman Red. After some soul searching, I opted to return the car to its original color. Again I would have been correct by NCRS standards if I had chosen any of the eight factory colors. But, to me, it just seemed right to return VIN #8027 to its original color.

There was no way to tell if the car originally had red or white coves. I painted the coves white on this car. Only approximately 30%-40% of 1959's had an offset colored cove. Offsetting colored coves are more indicative of the earlier 1950's, so the coves are done in the correct ermine white.

The color of the new paint was double checked by dipping a stirring stick in the new can of paint and holding it against a buffed portion of the glove box. This part of the exterior paint has been exposed to the least amount of sun and other elements and, therefore, after buffing, can reveal a "pretty close to original" shade of color.

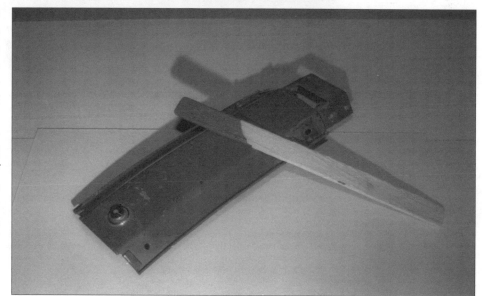

"Beauty of the Beast"

Chapter 5 — Painting

I have found no substitute for hard work and careful patience in the preparation and painting process. Mistakes are not covered by paint; they are amplified by paint. If a portion of this work is cheated, and a defect results, returning all the way back to the stripping and sanding stages will be mandated. It is better to do it properly from the beginning!

Seal the Fiberglass

The first step in the actual painting process is to prepare the body. When working with fiberglass you need to seal the body panels with a gel coat or feather fill type product. This step prevents the little strands of fiber from working their way through the paint with changes in temperature and heating effects of the sun.

Application of the gel coat also provides an opportunity to minimize all the little imperfections and waves in the body. You should not use a sanding block in this process as it will make your car too straight (better than factory original).

The feather fill product is sprayed on the body only after all the body repairs have been made. The application should be even over all parts of the car.

The doors and hood need to be bolted back in place using all new shims and weather stripping that will be used on the finished car. When the feather fill is sanded, the panels will be sure to match in a level fashion.

The car will appear to have "elephant skin" before all the ridges are sanded out. All the sanding should be done by hand with several pieces of sandpaper folded together allowing flexibility but minimize finger impressions in the body.

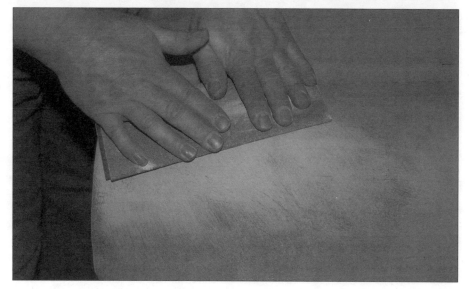

Do not block sand. It was not done with a block at the factory, and you will end up with a body that is too straight and even. In addition, a sanding block will get caught in the rounded curves of the body work. A little gouge caused by the edge of the block will cost much time to fix.

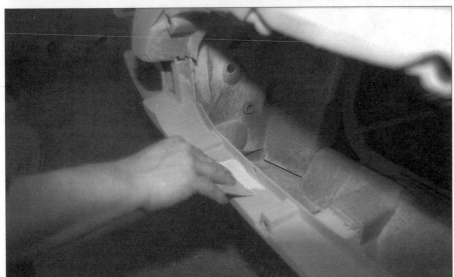

After the car has been sanded, tiny imperfections like cracks or noticeable low spots will be visible. Repair these with body filler.

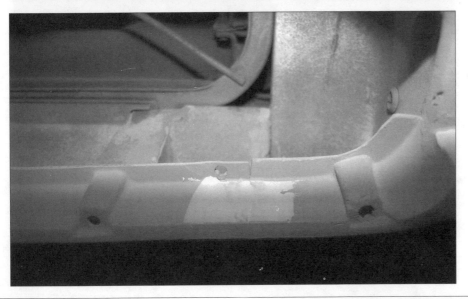

The body filler is applied with a plastic knife. It is best to use only enough filler to fix the depression or crack. Then sand the excess smooth to the body.

After the body has been sealed and smoothed in the feather fill process, the panels were taken back off the car for the priming and painting processes. The enemies of a perfect paint job are dust and loose debris. One can never be too cautious about removing dust and other foreign particles during the process.

Primer

The other big secret is using the right sandpaper. I strongly recommend 3M as it has the most consistent grain across multiple sheets. The car will be wet sanded after the primer has been applied using 300 to 600 grit sandpaper to remove any orange peel, bumps, or ridges in the primer coat.

A second layer of primer was sprayed on in thin coats. Again, this layer was sanded by hand without a sanding block. For this step you should use an even finer 600 to 1,000 grit paper.

Once the entire car as been primed and sanded for the second time you are ready to start the finish coat painting process. The following outlines the steps taken to achieve top-flight paint on our 1959 Corvette. We used polyurethane paint, but the steps are similar if you plan to use lacquer. However, you should wear protective clothing in addition to a respirator.

This body has had coats of primer applied twice and been sanded to a smooth even finish. Note how all exposed surfaces are primed.

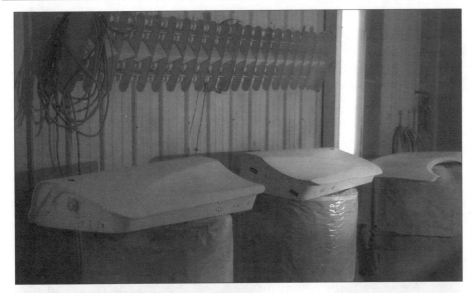

Each separate door and hood is removed from the car for the primer and finish coat painting processes. The parts are set on drums to make it easier to spray smooth even strokes without too much wear on the back.

Right before painting, use a tack cloth to remove any dust or loose primer.

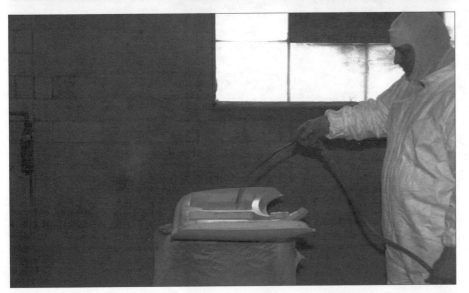

Blasting the area to be painted with air to make sure the surface is dry and again free from dust and other particles is always a good idea.

It is best to start spraying the edges first and work from one side of the panel to the other.

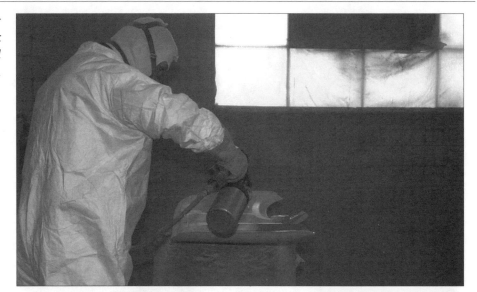

Place the panel or entire car body where you can spray from all angles. The last thing you want is to miss a spot because you could not see it properly.

The finished product is a paint that is smooth and dust free. The paint I used required 24 hours to dry. It is best to overcompensate with more drying time if you are unsure.

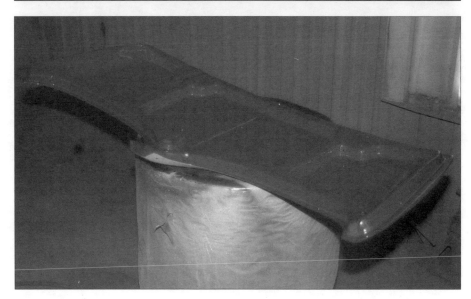

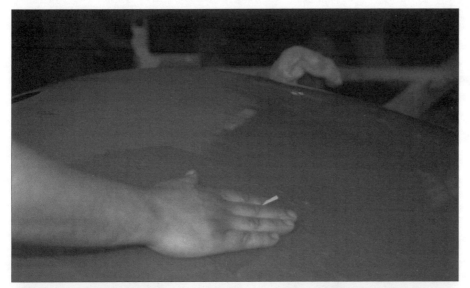

The dry paint is then wet sanded using 1,500-2,000 grit sandpaper. It is best to sand in circular motions until the tiny bumps (orange peel) are gone. It is extremely important not to sand too much of the paint off or scratch the paint too deeply.

The wet sand scratches are polished out using a very fine polishing compound and a sponge-like, foam buffing pad. Again, it is imperative that you do not polish through the paint down to the primer. Polish only long enough to remove the sanding scratches.

The last step buffs out the marks left by the polishing wheel. I used a clear glazing liquid and a cloth buffing wheel or glazing pad to buff the paint to a glass-like finish. The reflections in the paint should have a straight, not fuzzy, edge.

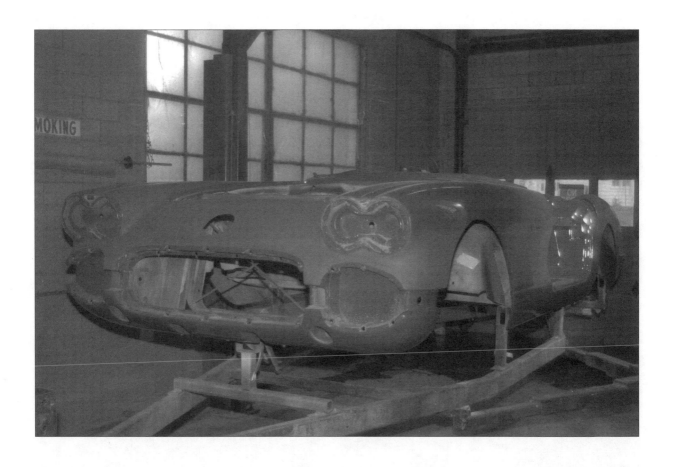

"Blasting Black"

Chapter 6 — Chassis Recondition

The frame is the foundation of the car. Fortunately, the frame on VIN #8027 was in excellent shape at the start of the restoration process. It had a little surface rust, but the metal had very little pitting or damage.

The early Corvettes had an X member that added strength and rigidity to the two beams that ran lengthwise. The fiberglass body and convertible body style conspired to require this added measure to make the car the strong performer on the track that it proved to be.

The best way to restore a chassis is to take the frame completely apart and dip the pieces in an acid bath. This requires that the pieces of the frame not only be unbolted, but that the seams be cut apart prior to dipping. Rust will exist between the parts and crevices. This is necessary because it is difficult for the acid to work its way between pieces that are welded together. Not only will rust still exist

Foundation

between the parts of the frame but the acid will have a difficult time drying from those little crevices thereby causing a white powder to form at those joints years later.

Acid dipping is a very difficult and expensive process. But, because the chassis was in such good shape at the beginning of the restoration process, an alternative was available to me. I was able to sandblast the frame and other chassis components. This process would ultimately save time and money, since the components of the frame did not need to be cut apart, and the parts did not have to be sent to an acid bath. Great care was taken to blast inside the frame and into all the seams. Every part that could be removed from the chassis was removed and blasted.

Another great advantage of being able to sandblast rather than acid dip is that the rivets and welded joints were not disturbed in the restoration process. Therefore, VIN #8027 was safe from the hazard of losing NCRS judging points because of an error in reassembling the frame.

Overall, sandblasting the frame seemed to be a logical method to use and a good way to hold down the cost of the restoration. On any budget, some choices need to be made about where to put restoration dollars. I am not advocating that all restorers follow the process described here, but sandblasting the frame was the better option for this car and for me than dipping the frame in acid.

In addition, the expert doing the chassis work was very comfortable with the sandblasting process and strongly recommended that course. Since it seemed to be consistent with my goal of making a top flight car, blasting was what I did.

Most of these parts will be reused in the restoration of the chassis. Note how straight and level the frame sits. This saves a trip in a frame jig to realign the four corners.

The next step in the chassis restoration process was to replace the components that were worn out or damaged. On any 35-year-old car, the rubber seals and bushings will be dry rotted. Parts that come into contact with fluids will also probably need to be replaced. Several kits are available to make parts selection less intimidating. For example, the easiest way to rebuild the front suspension is to buy a front suspension kit that includes all parts that normally wear out on a vintage car. Usually a restorer will need new rubber seals at front end tie rod connections to prevent the grease from leaking out of fittings. New bushings and tie rod ends will make the joints tight and result in a better driving car. Replacing the front springs was not necessary on my car as they were still holding the weight of the car properly and had no visible deterioration. However, since it is hard to evaluate springs visually, it may be best to replace them if there is any doubt.

Another kit that is a must is the body mount kit that contains correct rubber and fiber pads and other hardware. You should have already used a new mount kit before repairing the body.

Another extremely important part that should be replaced yet is often overlooked by restorers is the front end alignment shims. These go between the frame's side rails and the front suspension assembly. They were added to the Corvette frame in 1955 by Zora Arkus-Duntov to improve the handling of the car under hard driving conditions. (The shims changed the front end caster geometry.) They were one of the important changes that he made to the otherwise almost stock 1953 passenger car chassis.

After a preliminary cleaning, the parts need to be inspected for strength and integrity.

Another part that will almost surely need to be replaced is the battery tray. Until recently, an exact correct duplicate was not available. Incorrect trays will not be welded in the right spots and will have a slightly different configuration.

At the rear of the car routinely required replacements are simpler. In most cases the rear rebound straps will need to be replaced. Since those on my car were in good condition - just a little dirty - I kept the originals.

The exhaust system was replaced with aluminized pipes and components. There really is no sense in using stainless steel as it retains heat and discolors over time. Since it was not only incorrect but also twice as costly, I never seriously considered it as an option.

The underside of the frame looks as good as the top side after the project is completed.

Two different types of product are available to replace brake lines and fuel lines: stainless steel or plated. Stainless looks better, lasts longer, and people like it. In fact, some individuals have stated that stainless should be fully accepted as correct at NCRS judging meets. Their rationale is that stainless is a correct configuration, and it minimizes the need to replace these parts in the future.

But I had made a commitment to a goal. I set out to restore this car to its original specifications. Stainless was available in 1959, but there is no record that the car's designers and/or engineers ever intended these parts to be anything but plated. Therefore, I used plated hardware in all of these critical areas.

The finished product is nothing short of incredible even at the rear crossmember. The whole chassis has a smooth finish, free from pitting.

Rebuild the Chassis

Restoring the chassis requires lots of sandblasting, painting, and mechanical labor. This section outlines the steps you will need to take to rebuild the frame to NCRS specifications.

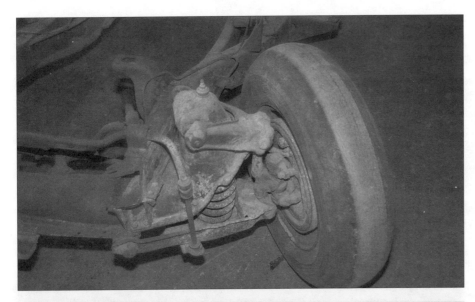

First, carefully remove the brake lines, gas lines, and other none structural, unusable parts. The car must be in bare frame form.

Sandblast the entire frame to remove most of the rust. It is important not to blast away healthy metal or cause pitting or scars in the surface.

When the surface rust is removed, it is much easier to take the chassis apart. This will expose all the hidden surfaces that will then be sandblasted. If you choose to dip your frame, the beams must be cut apart so that acid can enter and later dry from all surfaces otherwise acid will form a powdery residue at joints and cracks.

The rust free parts were then sprayed with rust retardant black paint. The key is to use paint that is not too glossy and not too flat. The assembled chassis is then rust-proofed with a rust retardant like 3M Rust Fighter. The application of this product should be generous as it will prevent future corrosive damage.

The brake lines and other components were put back on the frame. The chassis should be complete before engine, transmission, and body are reunited.

"Heart of the Machine"

Chapter 7 — Correct Engine

The motor is the essence of any true sports car. It separates the winners from the want-to-be's. The switch from underpowered 235 cid straight six(150 HP) to a more energetic 263 cid V8(195 HP) made the Corvette a true sports car in 1955. Corvette became a race winner in 1957 using an enlarged 283 cid engine with fuel injection (283 HP). In 1965, the optional 396 cid big block (with a thundering 425 HP) re-established the Corvette as an international class sports car.

Although not a milestone version, the engine in my 1959 Corvette is the relatively rare high performance version (270 HP). It was the second most powerful engine offered that year (fuel injection was rated at 290 HP), with about 18% more power than the standard engine (230 HP).

Three significant changes to the standard engine develop extra horsepower: 1. Carburetors; 2. Valve lifters; 3. Camshaft. By using dual quad carburetors instead of the standard single quad carburetor, the engine achieves better fuel and gas distribution to all eight cylinder chambers. Using solid or mechanical valve lifters in place of the standard hydraulic lifters, reduced valve float allowing the motor to rev to higher RPMs (revolutions per minute). The solid lifter engine did not red line until

The motor is the essence of any true sports car.

6,500 RPM's versus the standard hydraulic motor's 5,500 RPM redline. Lastly, Chevrolet's chief engineer, Zora Arkus-Duntov, designed a special high-lift camshaft. The lobes on this cam were designed to increase how long the valves were open (duration) and to increase how far they opened (lift). This design was possible only with the faster responding solid valve lifter's improved ability to more completely fill the cylinders (especially at high RPM's) with fresh air and fuel. The changes meant an engine could burn more fuel and thus produce more horsepower. The changes had a price. These cars can get as little as 14 MPG.

This motor, transmission, and rear axle assembly have been completely rejuvenated to original factory performance specifications.

The drivetrain, particularly the engine, presents to the restorer the widest range of options to upgrade or modernize a restored car. The choices range from inserting a new ZR-1 motor to restoring the correct block to its original performance and parts configuration.

My restoration philosophy was to return the car to what its developers had intended it to be. I have not reproduced production sloppiness, but I also have not used parts and technology not available in 1959. With this restoration perspective the decision not to insert a new ZR-1 motor was easy. After that, the choices became less black and white.

Without altering the original appearance of the engine, several improvements to the standard engine can be made (longer stroke crankshaft, bigger bore, or domed pistons). Even more visually obvious changes are tempting (electronic fuel injection or computerized ignition). However, these changes would go beyond the intended or designed performance of the time and therefore did not match my goals.

But, I did make one important exception. I made a change that will allow my Corvette to perform as originally intended with today's unleaded fuels. Unleaded fuels do not have the lubricating properties of the tetraethyl lead used in fuel 35 years ago. Burning unleaded fuel would eventually damage the valves and valve seats (valve seats are the area in the cylinder head that the valves close against). The solution was to use valves and valve seats that were made from a harder metal that could withstand the greater friction and the resulting higher temperatures. Using new cylinder heads was out of the question. The change would hurt the originality of an important component of the car. Instead, hardened valve seats were inserted in the original cylinder heads by drilling out the metal around where the valve meets the cylinder head and inserting a hardened metal ring to replace the softer metal that had been removed.

This chapter addresses correct drivetrain components. Chapter 8 addresses restoration to original performance specifications.

National Corvette Restorers Society (NCRS) and Corvette enthusiasts, in general, recognize the importance of the engine. Not only are the more powerful versions very rare, they are usually significantly more expensive. These factors make NCRS members and others carefully scrutinize these engines with an eye towards authenticity. Based on the assumption that the higher horsepower models are more valuable, the sport/hobby is interested in protecting the value of those very rare original high performance models. As a result, motors will receive an incredible amount of attention during verification and judging.

The rebuilt engine block is shown here ready for the cylinder heads, intake, and exhaust manifolds to be bolted in place.

The dual four barrel carburetors are mounted on the intake manifold and ready to be installed on the engine block once the cylinder heads are in place. The carburetors were cleaned and adjusted The next level of restoration would have meant replating and painting.

The general opinion is that the higher horsepower models are even more scarce than they were in 1959. Consider that fewer of the higher horse models were originally made and that a larger percentage of those were raced, it stands to reason that there are probably fewer remaining examples today. For example, of the 9,670 Corvettes built as 1959 models, only 745 (8%) of them had the high lift, fuel injected option (290 HP). Relatively few, 1,846 (20%) had the dual quad, high lift engine (270 HP). Considering that the higher horsepower cars were raced in greater percentages than the standard models, one would expect that less than 20% of the remaining cars today would be of the 270 HP variety.

My first step was to verify that the motor in VIN # 8027 was a correct engine. I would have no way to verify if this were the original engine as the VIN was not stamped on the engine pads until sometime in 1960. However, I could verify that the engine matched what would appear to be correct or typical for this car.

The engine is being run-in. In case there are problems with the rebuild, we will catch the problems before the body is dropped on the completed chassis. Note the garden hose that feeds cold tap water at a constant rate into the cooling system while the engine parts seat themselves.

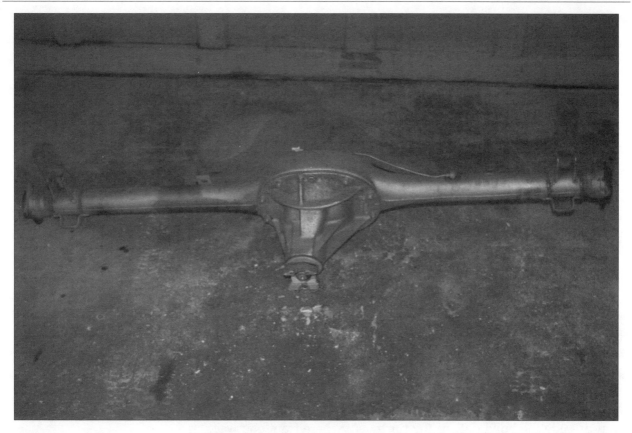

At this point the transaxle has been sandblasted, but it will need to have the spacers and seals replaced before we will call it "restored".

Without a VIN, I needed to use some deductive reasoning to confirm that this engine is correct for this car. First, because of the configuration of the frame and absence of holes in the firewall for automatic transmission safety lockout switch, I could be reasonably sure that the car originally had a manual, not an automatic, transmission. Automatic transmissions were not available with the higher horsepower cars which means any 1959 Corvette with an automatic transmission had to have a standard engine.

Second, my restorer and I checked the rear axle. A serial code, AN 0401, was stamped on the right front of the differential case. The code was difficult to read, but after removing the differential case cover, we confirmed that the rear axle gearing was 3:70/1 with positraction. The 0401 tells us that the unit was built April (fourth month) 1st. This transaxle was not available with an automatic transmission and usually came with high horsepower engines. Only 1,362 (15% of 1959 Corvettes) had this option.

The third indicator of the type of engine the car had was the transmission itself. The car has a 4 speed manual unit. In the upper left side of the transmission case is a code that reads W D 22 1, which tells us that this is a Warner 4-speed (W) built on April (D) 22nd, by the morning (1) shift. Again, this matched the type of engine currently in the car, so signs were strong that the motor was correct.

So far, we had been able to deduce that the car could have originally had a high horsepower unit, but we had not proved conclusively that it did. The best test of the "correctness" of this motor would be in the casting numbers and engine stamp on the engine itself. That will tell us a lot about when, where, and what kind of motor was originally built on this block. The first thing we checked was the engine block casting number which can be found on the top left surface at the rear of the block (firewall side). All 1959's had the casting number 3756519. This sort of information can be found in the NCRS judging manual for your car. After confirming the block casting number, check the block casting date The casting date can be found on the opposite side of the block from the casting number (right rear surface at the rear of the block). My block cast date read E 8 9, which means May (E) eight (8) of 1959 (9). The block casting date can precede the build date of the car by anywhere from one week to six months. However, in most cases the casting date is two or six weeks earlier than the car's build date. In VIN #8027, the casting date was three and one half weeks prior to the car's June 3 assembly date.

The Warner Gear Division T10 four speed transmission awaits the restoration bench.

After the engine block was cast it was sent to General Motor's Flint engine plant to be assembled to the desired horsepower configuration. When the engine was assembled, the block was stamped with information on where, when and what horsepower model was built. It is this engine pad stamp that is absolutely critical to determining the correctness of an engine.

On VIN #8027 the engine pad stamp in the front right upper corner of the block (just forward of the cylinder heads) reads F513CU. The (F) means the engine was assembled in Flint, which is correct for this year Corvette. The assembly date was May 13 (513), which was three working days after the casting date. One to seven days after the casting date is most typical. Lastly, the (CU) is the code for the 270 HP motor. Since this matches the carburetor units and cam/lifter setup, it appears to be correct.

The engine also appears to have the broach marks that were typical of factory production. Broach marks are the grinder scratches left in the metal when the block was decked (the top surface of the block was ground perfectly smooth and level to provide an airtight fit when the cylinder heads were bolted in place). The broach marks should run front to back and be perfectly straight.

All of these factors do not prove conclusively that these are the original drivetrain components, but we can be assured that they "could be" original. The proper term is what NCRS would call "correct" components. Another term that restorers and judges use is "typical".

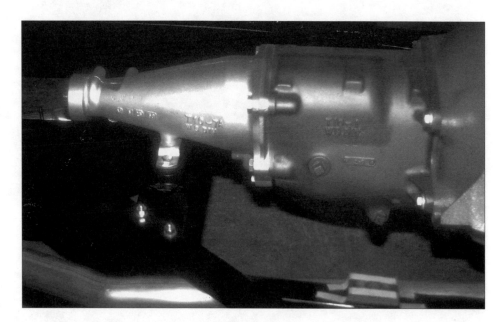

The transmission has been rebuilt on the inside as well as cleaned on the outside.

"Performance Original"

Chapter 8 — Drivetrain Rebuild

Now that we were confident that we were starting out with correct drivetrain components, my restorer could begin the process of bringing this 35-year-old has been from worn-out weakling to a like-new performer while being careful not to hurt the car's fit within NCRS standards. Although today's technology could make the engine stronger, smoother, and more powerful, great care was taken to restore the engine to its original performance specifications.

The best Corvette restorer is not the one who knows the most, has the most experience, or even has the best skills. The best restoration expert is the one who realizes what he does not know and cannot do. The skills and experience required for a drivetrain rebuild are quite different from the knowledge needed for body repair and paint work. During the restoration of the drivetrain, the motor was sent out to a specialist while the transmission and transaxle were not.

Quite extensive work needed to be done to rebuild the engine. The motor was completely rebuilt by a professional machine shop. Upon receiving the engine, the machinists disassembled it and cleaned each component with a strong acidic solvent sprayed through a high pressured nozzle in an enclosed cabinet. After they were cleaned, the parts were inspected for any visual flaws.

The Engine:

Visual inspection, however, will not reveal all defects. Cracks may exist that cannot be seen with the naked eye. The crankshaft, block, heads, and rods were Magnafluxed. This process electromagnetizes the part so that when a fluorescent solution containing iron particles is sprayed over it, any cracks will be seen as a break in the flow of liquid over the part. With the aid of black light the cracks show as bright lines. I was most fortunate that my engine was restorable.

The block was then checked for excessive cylinder wear and was found to need re-boring. The block was bored off the centerline of the crankshaft, (versus the less desirable off the deck method which only works if the deck is perfectly square to the centerline). After boring, the deck was checked for straightness and found to be within normal tolerances. If the block needed to be resurfaced, the decking process would have removed the critical engine pad stamping and left incorrect broach marks. Both are very bad in Corvette circles and would cost valuable judging points.

After the cylinders were bored, each was honed to achieve the appropriate cylinder finish and proper cylinder wall-to-piston clearance. During this process a cylinder head plate is torqued down on the deck to distort the cylinders in a way similar to the way cylinder heads would distort them. This improves the roundness that is achieved and helps allow for proper piston ring break-in.

The next component to be rebuilt was the crankshaft. After checking for wear and straightness, we found the crank on my engine needed to be ground to improve the roundness of the crank journals. Both main and rod journals were ground to meet proper clearance specifications required for appropriately oversized bearings. The rods were then also ground to the proper dimensions to mate with bearings and the crankshaft.

The block was ready for assembly which left the cylinder heads next in line for machine work. First, the exhaust valves were upgraded to stellate-faced valves. Although not critical, the intake valves were also replaced with new harder valves. Intake valves tend to run a little cooler due to the contact with cooler outside air. Bronze valve guides were installed for both exhaust and intake because they withstand the unlubricated properties of unleaded fuel better than the old steel valve guides.

The hardened steel-alloy exhaust valve seats were installed to prevent exhaust valve recession (the exhaust valve's wearing into the valve seat area). New springs, rocker arms, and stem-seals were installed to complete the head rebuild.

During final assembly, all clearances were rechecked, including the crankshaft and the piston ring end gaps. A new camshaft, identical in all specifications to the camshaft Dontov designed almost 40 years ago, was installed because the old one was badly worn. It is fairly typical that the cam lobes and lifters will show wear from the millions of times that they pushed against each other to open and close the valves.

With everything bolted back in place, including a new high volume oil pump, the engine was shipped back to the shop to be installed in the chassis and run-in. The run-in period would save much time later if the engine were not working properly. Lifting the engine out of the car over a fresh paint job once the body was in place would be very frustrating.

Unlike the engine, which was sent to a specialist, my restorer restored the transmission himself. The Borg-Warner transmissions, particularly the Warner T-10 four speed models, were tricky units. Many people replace them with a newer, easier-to-use Muncie unit and sacrifice the judging points. I opted to restore rather than replace the transmission.

Restoring a transmission involves several steps:

1. Examine the gears and replace those with worn teeth

2. Examine the sychromesh sleeves and replace worn rings

3. Replace all bearings, spacers and seals

4. Reassemble the parts with proper adjustments and linkage.

Though the tasks seem straight forward, a few elements of the process can only be learned through experience. It is not as easy as you might think to tell if the gears and sychromesh are worn. After carefully examining each component, we reassembled the unit with

Transmission and Axle Assembly:

what turned out to be a worn second gear. The worn gear caused it to pop out of engagement frequently. Also, the sychromesh was in bad shape which made it very difficult to downshift into second gear.

After discussing the problem with several experts, we determined the problem could be caused by the entire gear cluster's being improperly positioned within the casing. If the entire unit is too far back it prevents the shifter from fully engaging second gear. Not being fully engaged or engageable might cause the same problems as described above.

At this point we were not sure which elements were causing the transmission problems. My advice is to send the transmission to a transmission specialist. On the other hand, you might enjoy this sort of challenge.

The rear transaxle was rebuilt in the same manner. Its simpler design, however, required less expertise, and a restoration mechanic easily handled the work since nothing unique requiring special technical experience was involved. The unit on my car was in reasonable shape and only required new shims and seals.

The engine, transmission, and transaxle all represent unique challenges to restorers as they try to recreate a car that will perform as originally intended. The backyard mechanic should think twice before attempting to rebuild these components. In fact, the professional restorer should think about using the help of specialists. But, again, sometimes the fun is in trying.

This section outlines how this motor was restored to top condition by a professional engine shop.

The old 283 cid engine block has the correct casting number, casting date, and assembly pad stamp, but it needed a total rebuild to perform to original specifications.

First, check the block for any cracks, even ones that cannot be seen by the naked eye. The Magnaflux process gave an electrical charge to the block that created a magnetic field. By pouring a florescent liquid with iron particles over the entire block, inside and out, cracks can be detected as breaks in the magnetic field.

Second, bore the cylinder walls to a larger size (.016 inches). This allows for the old worn spots that were created by the rings and pistons from previous use to be eliminated, but does not change the performance characteristics of the engine.

Hold the block in place along the axis of its crankshaft. Line up the cylinders for boring by centering the boring bar (machine talk for drill bit) within the cylinder walls. Perfectly bored cylinders are created that are true to the crankshaft center and have the cylinder center in the precise same location as the old bore.

The third step is to hone the cylinders to remove any small imperfections in the surface of the cylinder wall left by the boring bar. This is such a precise task that a cylinder head plate is torqued to the top of the block before the procedure is started to simulate distortions caused when the cylinder heads are bolted in place. An additional .004 inches is removed with this process, making the combined bore/hone .020 inches larger than stock (20/1000 of an inch).

The honing machine polishes the inside cylinder walls with a constant stream of finishing oil to help reduce friction and cool the honed surfaces. Honing permits more precise sizing of the cylinder and a good "cross-hatch" surface needed for proper ring-to-cylinder sealing.

At the mid point of the honing process, the need for torquing the head plate in place is apparent. The bolts that hold the heads in place slightly pull the cylinders out of round at spots. The torque plate and its bolts allow for the same distortions to be replicated during the honing process.

Grind the crankshaft journals to remove any imperfections and ensure that the connecting rods and bearings have a smooth and perfectly round surface with which to mate. The crank is spun precisely on the axis of each journal until .020 inches are removed. Again, this will mate with the properly oversized bearings.

The oversized pistons (.020 inches larger than original) are installed on the rebuilt connecting rods (that again match the smaller crankshaft journals) which are held in place with new connecting rod bolts and bearings. The idea is to make sure that all the resurfaced areas are mated with appropriately oversized or undersized parts to properly compensate for the changes resurfacing created.

The cylinder heads will need to be rebuilt on even the most well preserved cars. Standard is to replace the valves and valve guides. This is usually where these engines start to lose their compression and performance characteristics.

With modern unleaded fuels, you must have hardened exhaust valves and valve seats installed to withstand the greater friction and heat created by the lack of lubrication in unleaded fuel. The valve seat area was drilled out to accept an insert that is made of much stronger steel thus allowing the use of unleaded fuels without causing engine damage.

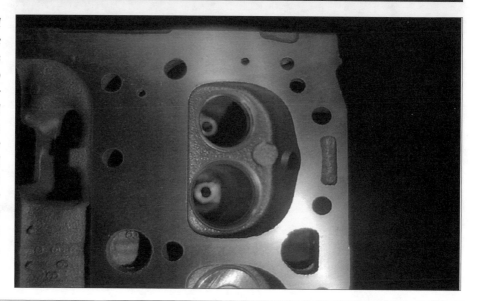

"Importance of Being Detailed"

Chapter 9 — Final Assembly

A worldly friend of mine, who knows nothing about Corvettes, asked a very simple question. "How can your Corvette be original when you have used reproduction parts to rebuild it?"

This question really cut to the heart of the final assembly matter.

Kit cars are not as valuable as the cars they emulate. Over restored or remanufactured cars are not prized as originals. The issue: how do you preserve an original when it has deteriorated over the course of 20 to 40 years?

With the chassis and drive train complete, the finished body is lowered into place. Great pains were taken to make sure that the body mount shims were in place and that the body would sit in the same position it had been in when the body was filled and painted. Thin strips of masking tape that hold the shims in place are left on the brackets after the mounting bolts have been tightened.

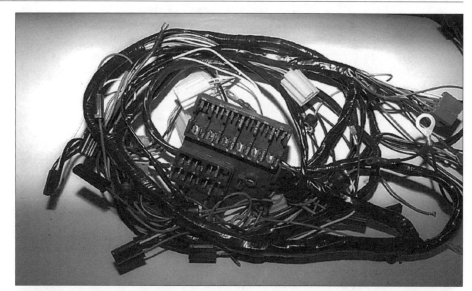

A new wiring harness is always a good idea. Not only could reusing old wires cause shorts and faulty electrical connections, but also a greater chance exists of having an electrical fire if old wires are worn or frayed.

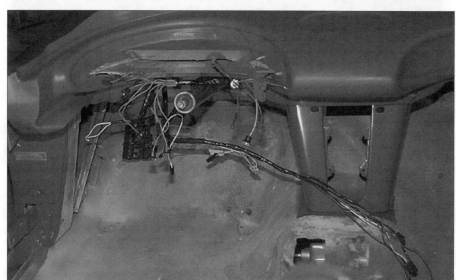

Before the final assembly can progress too far, all of the metal hinges and bolts will need to be sandblasted and re-plated with a nickel based galvanizing material. Special care should be given to make sure the color of the re-plating matches the color of the original plating. This color can range from an orange/brass to a silver, and the entire spectrum of hues covered the original parts seemingly without rhyme or reason.

In any restoration project, some key decisions need to be made that will affect the character of the finished car. I had already decided not to create a custom hot rod. Therefore, my range of choices became focused on how strictly I chose to interpret the word "original."

Choices seemed to fall into three categories:

1. Exact; return the car exactly as it was built, including both design defects and production flaws.

2. Intended; return the car to its intended state, not changing design or components but correcting production sloppiness.

3. Improved; return the car to the condition it should have been in when it was built, even using improved parts to correct obvious design flaws.

Using the improved strategy would allow a restorer to replace the parts that never seemed to work right even when brand new. Like most vintage cars, Corvettes had a few flaws, including heat vent dampers and clocks. Many parts suppliers sell re-engineered components and are very clear not to represent them as original specification parts.

In my case, a lot of care had been used to make sure this car was just like it would have been when it rolled off the assembly line 35 years ago. My goal, Choice #2, was to restore VIN #8027 to the "original" condition as "intended" by the car's designers.

When an original Corvette is restored, the goal is to reverse its deterioration: to preserve the car and the memory of the car. We want to remember these cars in their prime, rather than neglected relics.

Restoration may sound straight forward, but to accomplish it is harder than one might realize. The degree to which one achieves a goal depends on the ability to discern detail. The sport of the hobby is in the level of care taken during the final assembly process.

Some of the metal parts, like this door hinge, will need to be brazed to repair the rusted through areas. It is better to sandblast all the rusted metal away even if it results in additional brazing work.

The brazed part should be bolted in place to ensure that it fits properly before it is painted.

The hinge shown here is identical to the hinge as it would have appeared from the factory. Note the glue slop on the weather strip next to the hinge. All original cars had significant amounts of glue showing as the glue was applied with a brush in a rushed manner.

Key decisions revolve around which parts to replace and which parts to restore. Since my objective was to return this Corvette to its intended condition at the time of manufacture and dealer preparation, I used a combination of refurbished original parts as well as top quality reproduction parts. I made the decisions part by part, as issues arose. If the original was in good condition or easily cleaned/rebuilt, I used the original part. If the original was in bad shape I looked for a reproduction part.

In the case of Corvettes you can buy almost every part needed to build an authentic reproduction of an early Corvette. You can even order a General Motors VIN tag if the one for your car had been lost.

But, a cost parameter needs to be considered. Although replacement seat belts ($600) and voltage regulators ($500) are available, the cost did not seem worth the value they represented to the overall car. You might consider using a part that will come close to representing an authentic part (not totally unlike original) and saving your resources to spend on the components that are the most important to you. Later, the parts can always be upgraded if you decide to go for more points.

At least one of the major Corvette supplier, has cataloged every part needed to build a 1957 Corvette. Every single part is available, some original, some fairly close. This is a terrific feat testifying to how vigilant parts suppliers have become in finding exact reproductions of original Corvette parts.

So, how can you tell an original from a pretender? I refer back to the first chapter where I suggested buying a National Corvette Restorers Society Judging Manual. A manual is written for every era of car. The book will outline in incredible detail exactly what original parts and trim should look like. The Judging Manual contains more than 100 pages of diagrams and other details.

The Judging Manual is a good place to start the research process when planning which parts to restore and which to replace. It will also serve as a good tool for repairing old, worn parts. NCRS also prints very detailed research articles in Corvette Restorer Magazine.

After you have read the Judging Manual, you will need to come to philosophical terms with the inclusion of replacement parts before starting the final assembly of your restored car. Does your goal call for exact reproduction parts, or will you use improved-design parts?

The radiator is lowered in place after the engine is bolted in and the body is lowered back.

The fender spears are held in place with posts that poke through the fiberglass fenders. The stainless is held in place with self tapping speed nuts that are twisted onto the posts.

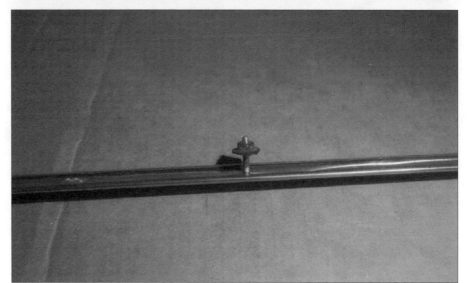

I chose to try to use as many original cleaned/rebuilt parts as possible and to use only parts that were exact reproductions of original parts. This perspective fit with my restoration goal of returning the car to its original condition as intended by the car's designers without the production warts. Therefore, I did not use improved parts, but I did not replace the production sloppiness like overspray on the gas cap.

I did not use a chrome molding when stainless was intended and original. I also did not use better, modern fasteners in place of the hard-to-find old ones. The NCRS Judging Manual for 1959's gave me very valuable information for evaluating how parts appeared as original. Most clubs for specific models of cars offer some sort of technical guidelines. I was fortunate that Corvettes have one of the most progressive and organized clubs and provide technical help in a generous manner.

Another good practice is to save any parts no matter how broken or worn they appear to be. Although you may be able to find a replacement part, having the old original part for comparison will provide another opportunity to verify the replacement's size, shape, material, finish, configuration.

For example, 1958-60 Corvette rear light lenses are available from suppliers. They are properly dated and correct in every way, but the little stainless trim that bisects the lens will be slightly different from the original. An astute restorer who had saved his old broken lenses can remove the trim strip from the old lens and apply it to the new lens.

Another key to the final assembly process is to find the right parts suppliers. Some suppliers are as detail oriented as NCRS judges. They share the ability to notice even the tiniest deviations from original parts.

Price is not a good criterion to use in picking a parts supplier. You will lose time and money replacing wrong parts or buying new ones if the ones you receive are defective.

Many excellent parts suppliers are honest and can tell you when a part is correct or merely close to being correct. Another thing to look for in a parts supplier is the range of parts he carries. It is somewhat easier to deal with one major supplier than several little ones.

These are perfect reproductions of the original headlight lens, but current laws require a Department of Transportation approval, so this glass has a tiny "D.O.T." under the stainless trim. A judge will know it is there just like the hard-to-detect D.O.T. on the tires.

These are correct tail lamp lenses marked with the Guide RIC 58. The lenses are dated the year preceding manufacture on most vintage cars. The mold was made in 1958 when the 1959's started production in the fall of that year.

This is an original hubcap. Excellent quality reproductions are available that are virtually indistinguishable from the originals. Spinners are sold separately and can be replaced.

Detail is even important in the installation of the exhaust pipe system. The pipe in this Figure extends even with the chrome bumper and, therefore, protects the bumper from being discolored by the car's exhaust.

The pipe in this Figure is only a sixteenth of an inch (.062) shorter but leaves exhaust soil on the chrome bumper, because it does not quite extend beyond the edge of the chrome.

The gas cap is a reproduction unit as is the other hardware in the gas filler compartment. A few points will be lost for not having the proper overspray, but the neat job is consistent with the "as intended" objective set at the beginning of the project.

By today's standards the fit of the stainless components was not very good. The chrome headlight bezels were always higher than the stainless trim that was designed to tuck underneath the chrome lip.

The pieces were designed to fit together in a sturdy fashion, but again, as this cove molding shows, it was not a seamless design.

One of the hardest elements to replace correctly in a restoration project is the window felt. The stitching in the window jam is very hard to replicate. Also, the felt must be tight enough to provide a snug fit but not so snug that the window does not roll up and down properly.

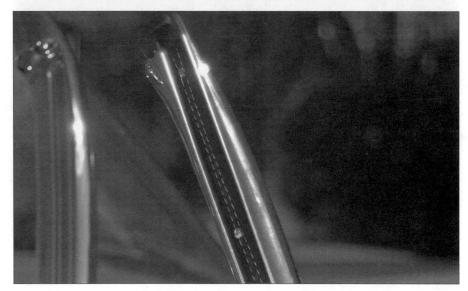

A number of good suppliers in the Corvette business, were born of necessity. Twenty years ago Jerry Kohn was restoring a 1958 Corvette and was frustrated to learn that the replacement parts being sold were made of cast aluminum, which was not only incorrect but resulted in very poor chrome quality. Jerry went to work creating grill teeth made of the proper Zinc Diecast material for Corvettes built between 1953 and 1961. Incidentally, the same teeth, with different sequences and combinations for each series, were used in all eight years. The disadvantage of Zinc diecast teeth is that when moisture gets under the chrome the metal begins to pit. The aluminum might be considered an improvement if they were not so soft and dent prone. Regardless, a purist looking for exact reproduction parts requires zinc not aluminum.

Today, quality parts suppliers manufacture dozens of parts that cannot be found in boneyards or from General Motors. For example, GM made replacement hood and decklid emblems for Corvettes, but the lettering was silver instead of the original gold. Various lore can be heard that they were all originally silver but the original ones were bleached gold by the sun. Or perhaps GM wanted to differentiate between original and replacement using the traditional second place color instead of first place gold to signify the emblem as a replacement part.

Another mark of a good supplier is his return policy. When ordering hundreds of parts, even the best suppliers are going to miss a defect now and then. In my case it was a rear deck lid soft cover latch. After a few uses the rivets came loose on one of the latches.

I called the supplier and explained the problem. To my amazement, instead of skeptical questioning, I received an apology for any inconvenience and was promptly given a return authorization number and instructions for returning the defective part in exchange for a new one which I received in the mail only 10 days after sending the defective one back.

Exterior pieces like the side view mirror are likely to take a beating over the years and will most likely need to be replaced. This is a refinished original example. The difference is in the round swivel that fits into the mirror piece. The reproduction units are elongated instead of round.

Interior parts, like the rear view mirror, are usually in better shape than exterior detail pieces.

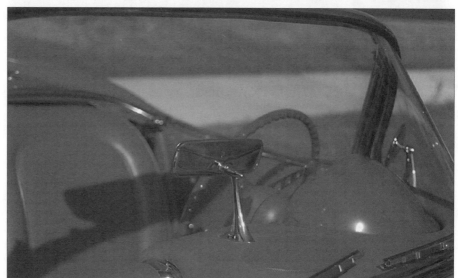

If you look closely behind the chrome grill teeth, the bolt that holds the teeth to the crosspiece is the proper length, about 1 inch longer than the bracket. Reproduction bolts that are a quarter inch longer detract from the originality of the car.

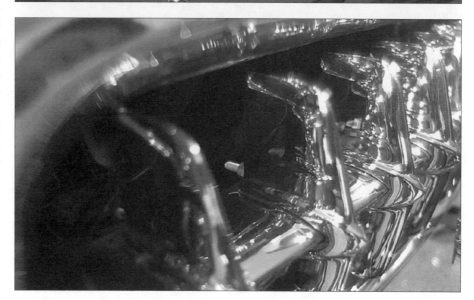

The interior of the Corvette is such a specialized area that it should be treated a little differently. The technology used to develop vinyl and carpet reproductions is very different than the technology used to reproduce the metal and plastic components.

The source I used was known for supplying authentic vinyl and carpet components for 1953 through 1989 Corvettes. Perhaps the secret to their success is the attention to detail they are able to give because they are focused on doing interior parts only. Being an expert in one niche of the Corvette replacement parts market is easier than trying to meet all needs.

Regardless of the source, the little details that make an interior an authentic reproduction are the thickness of the vinyl, the grain and color, and the manner of its construction. For example, in 1959 the vinyl used was much thicker than the vinyl used in mid-year cars of the sixties. A good interior supplier will form the vinyl's grain, pattern, and form by using a Di-electric machine. This machine was used to make vinyl for early cars by shooting 100 kilowatts of microwave molecules through the vinyl to mold it into proper shape and bond it to the foam backing. This ensured that the vinyl graining would look and wear like the old sturdy fabric of 35 years ago. It is also a plus to have real latex foam rubber instead of the modern polyurethane type foam.

The correct carpet is even more difficult to achieve as it requires that the supplier go through several difficult steps to reproduce the material, color, and weave that has long been out of style. The yarn fabric itself needs to be specially woven to match old standards that include raw materials, like rayon, that are not popular now. Once the correct yarn is produced, it is woven to the proper density and weave style. Throughout this process, the color is matched to the original specifications for that year's car.

Unlike the engine and exterior components that were often repeated for several years, the interior parts were usually changed every year. Since new styles and colors and materials were introduced annually, only top suppliers have the capability to stock all the variations for each year. Again, I caution restorers to choose your dealers and suppliers with care.

One final note: it is the careful research in reproducing parts the way they were originally made that allows a restorer to bring a car back to its original condition. The key is to be as detail-specific as possible. The pains and efforts expended here will differentiate your car - a true masterpiece - from one that is merely a nice restoration.

Sometime in mid-1959 the mounting bracket for the radio speaker was redesigned. The configuration shown here was the later design that did use the metal trim ring around the speaker grill.

Note how the dash pad is pre-formed to fit around the fiberglass.

The interior is completely disassembled and ready to be cleaned, stripped, and rebuilt.

The instrument cluster has been rebuilt with refinished gauges. Some charming ideosyncracies include a speedometer that is almost 10% faster than the actual speed and a temperature gauge that always reads hot because the temperature sending unit is the wrong ohms. Incidentally, currently no one makes a proper sender unit, but several suppliers are working on developing one. Note the 6,500 red line on the tachometer which is correct for a solid lifter engine.

Corvettes had one of the first signal seeking radios. The units were called Wonderbars for the button that was pushed to actuate the seeking mechanism. Note the chrome trim around the edges of the radio/defroster console. The smallest detail, including the type of screw used, is important when the car appears on the judging field.

The passenger side grab bar has been recovered with vinyl that matches that on the dash pad. The Corvette badge on the cove area signifies this is a 1959 interior as differentiated from the 1958 and 1960, each of which is distinctly different.

The care taken during the fiberglass repair and painting stages will pay off in the final assembly. By sanding, filling, and painting with the doors, hood, trunk, and other panels in place, gaps will be perfect. The same weatherstrip that was used in the sanding and painting process needs to be used in the final assembly process. Notice how the trunk is level with the rear deck and soft top cover.

Also the door and the gas tank cover match the body side because care was taken to reuse the same weatherstrip.

The lines looking down the side of the car are equally straight and true.

"Why Are We Here?"

Chapter 10 — Judging Field

Nothing can prepare you for your first trip to the judging field. A large part of your life will be scrutinized by others for the first time. You have put a lot of yourself and spent precious time and money getting your car ready for this day.

The fact that my first show experience was at Bloomington Gold, one of the largest shows in the country, did nothing to alleviate my first day jitters. Nor were my nerves soothed by the situation that the first time I saw the completed car was on the judging field. I was only able to review the last details of the restoration project as the judges approached. The world would read about the final outcome of this event.

Basically, I broke every guideline for having a successful show. Mac Johnson, the Chief Judge at Bloomington Gold, later explained his theories on the subject. He is a particularly good advisor because of his expertise in judging. But, he also has made ensuring that participants in the Bloomington event have an enjoyable experience his top priority.

His theory is based on what engineers call the "fire triangle" which is created when all three elements (oxygen, heat, and a combustible material) necessary for fire to occur are present. Johnson refers to an "enjoyment triangle" for having a successful car show. If any one of the three elements is missing, the participant's potential for having a good experience dwindles to almost impossible.

The three elements for a successful show are:

1. The car should be finished well in advance of the show.

2. The owner should focus on preparing himself for the show by reading materials, understanding the judging perspective, and being familiar with the event's procedures.

3. The owner should bring a positive attitude. Do not be defensive or rigid. This is not life or death.

At Bloomington the cars are sorted by year/class and are judged by teams of four experts.

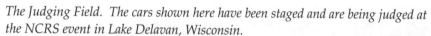

The Judging Field. The cars shown here have been staged and are being judged at the NCRS event in Lake Delavan, Wisconsin.

Putting my disastrous "maiden voyage" behind me, I was determined to avoid the same mistakes the second time around. I finished the car properly, studied my NCRS materials (both 1958-60 Judging Manual and Judging Reference Manual) and came to the show with my family determined to have a fun weekend and learn a bit about Corvettes.

That was the spirit I brought to the NCRS event at Lake Delavan, Wisconsin, one month later. What a difference! The "enjoyment triangle" is good advice for anybody.

In addition to Mac Johnson's advice, the following are my suggestions for taking a car to any technically-oriented car show. First, these shows are not cleaning contests so there is no need to worry about getting that last speck of dust from the corner of the windshield. Remember, the purpose of the show is to convey an understanding of how closely the car in question represents the car as it came off the assembly line.

Knowledge gained is more important than the score

Second, each show is a learning opportunity. Come prepared with a list of questions you want to ask the judges or other knowledgeable people. Distracting the judges while they are judging is not a good idea, but there is usually time for questions after they have familiarized themselves with your car.

Third, get to know other owners of cars like yours. They are likely to have experiences similar to yours and can provide valuable information about how they solved problems during the restoration process.

In other words, the show is a chance to learn, not an end in itself. The score is not so important as the knowledge gained during the process of the event. I need to repeat this, the score is not as important as the knowledge gained during the event.

Learn more about your car. Enjoy the experience. Have fun with it. Ask lots of questions.

The event at Lake Delavan was wildly successful. My family had fun. I learned an incredible amount about my car. In fact I received 31 separate suggestions about steps I could follow to make VIN #8027 more authentic! Now the question became: which information/input do I use immediately?

Dennis Clark, National Judging chairman of NCRS, was asked to comment on the results of the Lake Delavan event. The following letter contains his ideas on what I could do with the suggestions from the judging sheets. Very informative, the advice is given in a friendly (often joking) manner.

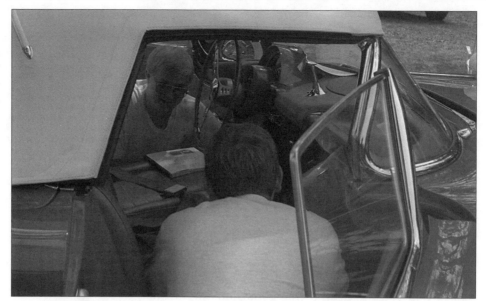

The two NCRS judges review each item as described in the NCRS Judging Manual for that class car. Note how the judges are referring to the manual during the process.

Paul,

Overall your car did very well. You earned a top flight award but more importantly you learned some things that will help you make a better car.

OPERATIONS:

Wonderbar Radio -3 pts., could be an expensive fix. At -3 I might let it ride unless you feel another judge might turn this into a -12. This could be a little risky if the signal seeking feature simply does not work.

Heater & Defroster -6 pts., I'd fix this. Whatever the problem is, it should be fairly easy and inexpensive. I'd want it to work anyway.

Fire Extinguisher, no excuse here. You need to go buy one. The 3 bonus points would have covered the radio and whether you drive your car or not, have one just in case you need to save your car or someone else's.

Be thankful your car does not have windshield washers!

Overall on Operations, -9 pts. Not bad, but did the operations team do a pretty thorough job, or did you "get by" with something that really needs to be addressed?

A serious player strives for 100% , plus 3 bonus points, on the operations area. This is basically non-subjective and these points are the ones you should count on to make up for the little surprises down the line.

INTERIOR:

Seat Belts, -6 pts. Expensive fix and a big dollar decision on whether to replace or not. Might let it ride for now.

Carpeting, -3 pts., sounds like you had the seats bolted through on top of the carpet. Oops, easy fix but you are stuck with some holes in the carpet and possible chaffing, but it might not be too noticeable.

Defroster, -3 pts. Sounds like you have the steel replacement heater distribution box rather than the nice reproduction original heavy cardboard style. Think I'd get the correct one, even though they seem a little expensive. Judges invariably catch this one.

Glove Box Rubber Bumper, -1 pt. About a $4 fix, and judges love to see this in place. It takes about 10 seconds to install.

Jack "Repro Tube", -2 pts. No excuse for not having removed this. Shame on you.

Tire Tools -25 pts. How could you have been so silly? Spend big bucks for the jack and not stepped up the reasonably priced tools? Will you ever learn....(read your judging manual)? No excuse for not having these in place before the next judging meet.

On the interior and trunk, -55 pts. Well if you'd have "stepped" up for the tire tools, removed that stupid jack tube, and not installed the seats on top of the carpet, this could have been only a -20. Boy that sounds better.

EXTERIOR:

Body Paint, "Urethane/No Orange Peel", -20 pts. Uncertain "danger area" here. Judging Manual allows for up to a full deduction for "obvious" non-lacquer paint, so this area could be subject to a possible 50 point originality deduction at future events. This in itself will not prevent achieving a Top Flight Award, but we have to be prepared if that big hit comes along.

What we do here is to strive to make the rest of the car good enough to overcome that as-manufactured deviation and potential point deduction. If you plan to drive your car, maybe the non-factory type paint is the best way to go. It becomes a trade off type decision.

Headlamps, -5 pts. Think I'd chase down the correct model headlamps. Maybe spend the dollars to buy some at a wrecking yard. Who knows what other treasures you might find.

Tires, -12 pts. Well, this is a toughy. The original style reproduction bias ply tires should only receive a 3 point deduction. An example of not knowing the Judging Reference Manual. Judges are human and can make mistakes. Knowing the rules could have saved you the extra 9 point deduction.

On exterior, -44 pts. All originality points, no deducts on condition so it sounds like the judges liked what they saw. If you are "at ease" with the paint issue, finding the headlamps and knowing the tire rules saves you 14 points for a net loss of only 30 in this section.

MECHANICAL:

Valve Covers, glassbeaded, -5 pts. Think we should send these babies off to one of the places that specializes in aluminum refinishing. They do a real good job, not too expensive, and are one of the most prominent items the judges have to look at when the hood comes up.

Exhaust Manifolds, No Orange Overspray, -5 pts. Well, well. I know it's hard to bring ourselves to do it, but since we didn't do it right the first time when it would have been easy, you have to go through the misery of removing or carefully masking to get the paint where it needs to go. At least very little expense here, just a philosophical decision. Think you should check a few other cars which were done correctly to see exactly where we need to carefully apply that paint.

Fan Belt, Service Replacement, -2 pts. Good reproductions are now available. Think I'd step up. Might use the present one for driving or as a backup.

Fan Shroud Bolts, -2 pts. Cheap fix here. Let's do it while installing the fan belt.

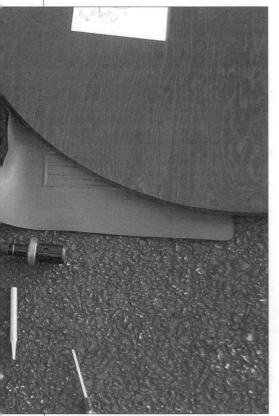

Voltage Regulator, -6 pts. No fire alarm, but you should be on the lookout for the correct item. The one we need can be expensive but with a little patience and persistence you can eliminate those nagging 6 points which the judges will always catch.

On mechanical, -29 pts. Good show on mechanical if the judges were knowledgeable and experienced. I'd think we were in pretty good shape here.

SUMMARY:

Overall on the car, -137 points and a solid Top Flight car at 96.9 percent net. Great score by any measure!

Apparent Strong Points: Judges seemed to like the condition, the car must look pretty darn good. Did quite well in all areas of the judging with almost no big areas of concern that can't be addressed with comparative ease and acceptable expense.

Apparent Weak Points; Based on the score sheets, the only danger area is the paint type. If the other items are fixed, even a full 50 point deduct on paint originality would result in the same total point level. And I think you could live with that.

The Unknown; Because of the different judging skill levels encountered from meet to meet, you need to decide if you want your car to undergo further scrutiny at those "higher levels". If you enjoyed the participation and want to learn more about your car, it's a good idea to try and attend one of these events. Not only will having your car judged again help, but studying the other cars at these events and talking with the judges and other owners always provides a productive exchange of knowledge for those who seek it. And maybe, more importantly, you're going to meet some other members who may become friends, sharing in this fun and fascinating hobby.

- Dennis Clark

Of the 31 suggestions I received from my NCRS judges at Lake Delavan, some suggestions were very straight forward while others required additional research. An example of a straight forward item is that my seats were incorrectly installed on top of the carpet. Some more difficult issues were raised about the windshield washer, speaker grill, and carpeting. I will have to do more research before deciding to implement those suggestions. For instance, my car did not have the windshield washer option; however, the

Never stop learning

washer pump is still in place on the car. Both the judge at NCRS and the judge at Bloomington deducted points for the washer pump on the windshield wiper motor. The difference lies in the advice each judge gave me regarding the pump. The pump should either not be on the wiper motor at all, or the pipe should be crimped depending on which judge's advice you took.

To resolve the dilemma, I consulted Nolan Adams Restoration book (no answer) and the NCRS Judging Manual (no help). Finally, I contacted a knowledgeable NCRS expert, Robin Winnan, who was able to resolve the issue. His experience with original Corvettes was overwhelmingly in favor of the washer pump being totally removed from the wiper motor.

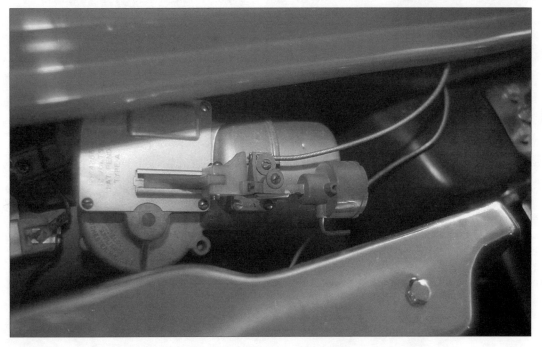

Should this windshield wiper pump stay or go? The experts say it should be removed.

The speaker grill presented another conundrum. Currently my speaker grill is the 1958 through mid 1959 variety. The grill is raised from the dash about an eighth of an inch and does not have a trim ring bezel around it. At both shows I received full points for having the proper speaker grill configuration.

The NCRS Judging Manual identifies that the speaker grill was changed late in the 1959 model run to the later style 1960-62 grill. However, the manual is not specific about exactly when the change took place. To find more information, I consulted the Winter 1994 edition of *The Corvette Restorer* Magazine that carried an article presenting the careful research about exactly when and how the change was made. It seems that the fiberglass dash around the speaker grill was changed from a design that required the speaker to be installed from under the dash to a system that allowed the speaker to be installed from the top side of the dash. Instead of screws protruding down from the fiberglass to accept the speaker from below, the new style had holes drilled that allowed the pins protruding from the trim ring to hold the speaker in place. After examining the photographs of my car taken during the restoration process, I discovered that I have the newer style fiberglass configuration and, therefore, should switch to the trim ring style grill. Because research is still being done on this topic, I will wait a few months before making the adjustment.

Although this speaker grill was judged to be correct by judges at both shows, I suspect the newer style with the trim ring bezel would be authentic.

I was also curious about the carpet style. I received full credit for the Daytona style carpet in my car. However, at both shows I attended, the cars next to me also received full credit with completely different carpet! Some people believe the style of carpet changed some time in very late 1959 from the pure red carpet with short loops (Daytona style) to a red and black carpet with longer loops (Tuxedo style). The cars restored with Tuxedo style were produced three weeks before and two weeks after mine. To resolve this question, I consulted Al Knoch who claims that although it is popular to use the Tuxedo carpet in very late 1959's, only the Daytona red carpet is correct. He has never seen a verified example of Tuxedo style carpet in a 1959 Corvette and believes the misinformation was started several years ago when the first Corvette catalog mistakenly listed the Tuxedo style as the correct style for 1959.

This is correct Daytona carpet for 1959 Corvettes, but it should be installed over not under the seat frame bolts and brackets.

Bloomington versus NCRS

Many people have asked me how the Bloomington Gold and NCRS events compare. This is a very easy question to answer. They are almost identical in their purpose and style.

Both organizations focus on having participants enjoy the experience through learning more about their car's original configuration. They both award points or deduct points for items that are not thought to represent an original Corvette.

The percentage of points assigned to various areas of the car are more similar than not. The following chart compares the percentages by area.

Percentage of Judging Points by Area

Components	Bloomington	NCRS
Interior/trunk	25%	22%
Exterior/body	23%	23%
Mechanical/engine	28%	39%
Chassis	17%	—
Operations/technical	7%	16%

The engine compartment is probably the most scrutinized area of the entire car.

"Enjoy Your Car"

Chapter 11

The last thought I will leave with you is: enjoy your car. Do what you want. Drive it!

Two pieces of equipment that every Corvette owner should have regardless of whether the car is restored or not are a good car cover and a polishing/buffing machine.

While the vast majority of car covers come from a very few suppliers, one can purchase them at literally hundreds of locations. I tested covers from several suppliers as well as those made from the two major types of material (cotton and paper).

To evaluate the covers, I first reviewed why I wanted a cover in the first place, which was to protect the car from such hazards as the children's bumping against it or a garden tool's falling on the car. Certainly a cover is essential to keep some of the dust off the car. I even went so far as to build a wall in my garage so that the amount of traffic that can come close to my car is minimized.

Children's occasional resourcefulness is frightening

But as anyone with children can attest, their occasional resourcefulness is frightening. Therefore, I evaluated the covers using three criteria:

1. Which provided the most protection?
2. Which fit the car snugly?
3. Which extended all the way down below the hubcaps?

Although your needs might result in different priorities, I chose a cotton/flannel car cover in which the cotton seemed to be thicker and softer than that in the other brands I tested. The cover also fit my car significantly better than other covers tested, including covering the car all the way down below the wheel spinners on the hubcaps. The manufacturer is smaller than many and has limited distribution, so you may have to work to find the same cover.

This is a 100% cotton car cover that has a flannel finish inside. It fits snugly and covers all the way down to the hubcaps.

The second piece of equipment you should own is a high quality car buffer. An electric buffer will allow you to polish your car faster and with less energy than doing it by hand. It will also help you do a better job because the polish will be worked into the paint better, and you will not lose interest in the project as quickly as you might if you were hand buffing.

Again, I tested various models, looking for one that would not leave swirl marks or damage the paint. The key is to find a machine that oscillates in a natural motion and at a relatively slow speed. Professional units can go as fast as 3,000 to 9,000 RPM's which is much too fast for home car care needs. The machine is so fast and powerful that a novice can very easily polish right through the paint.

A buffer like this is essential for properly working the polish and wax into the paint finish.

I am so committed to enjoying my car that I commissioned a supplier to make a special driver's seat for me that would give me more head room. Since I am 6'3", my head hit the roof when I sat in a standard seat. My custom seat looks exactly like an original, but it is 3 inches lower than standard. I can pop the original seat back in place for shows in a matter of seconds. In the meantime, the ergomomics of my car are improved, and I enjoy it even more.

This special seat is correct in every detail exept the frame is 3 inches lower, which allows me to sit more comfortably with more head room. I put the original in if VIN #8027 is being entered in judging events.

*Part of enjoying a car is
just looking at it.*

Appendix

Two sources stand out as absolutely irreplaceable for anyone planning to restore a vintage car. First, membership in a club specializing in the specific model you are interested. Clubs usually bring a wealth of expertise and experience that are very helpful to the beginner and old-pro alike. Second, a good source for finding cars and parts for your make vintage car. The local newspaper does not have a broad enough coverage and most magazines are not specific to restorer's needs.

The two sources I used were the National Corvette Restorer's Society and *Corvette Trader and Chevy's* Magazine. The information below tells you what they offer Corvette fanatics and how to contact them.

National Corvette Restorer's Society

The club is the largest source for Corvette information of any year. They offer Judging Manuals, Technical Manuals, Magazines and free advice from knowledgeable members. The Judging Manual for your specific year Corvette is probably the best source of information you can have. NCRS does have a strong preference that you be a current member or join when you purchase your Judging Manual. This allows them to forward revisions and updates.

Contact: Gary or Eric Mortimer,
NCRS,
6291 Day Road,
Cincinnati, OH 45252-1334
phone: (513) 385-8526, fax: (513) 385-8544

Corvette Trader and *Chevy's* Magazine

The magazine is by far the largest Corvette publication in the world. It is also the most comprehensive source for Corvettes for sale and Corvette parts. No other publication has as many cars, parts or services in a single issue.

In addition, they publish a Mustang/Ford Trader and a mammoth Old Car Trader that features hundreds of vintage makes and models. All are available at newsstand or through subscription.

Contact: *Corvette Trader and Chevy's,*
P.O. Box 9059,
Clearwater, FL 34618-9059
phone: (813) 538-1800, fax: (813) 535-4000

Car Evaluation Worksheets

The previous chapters outline the principles I used to make the restoration decisions on my car, a 1959 Corvette that started out in pretty rough shape. Each car is different, but the important decisions are remarkably similar.

These three sections are designed to help you transfer the experience of VIN #8027 to your project car. The three valuable worksheets are:

Restoration Objective Worksheet

Read these 20 statements and record your agreement/
disagreement with them. They are designed to help you think through
the purpose and role that restoring a car will serve in your life.

1 disagree - agree 5 to the following statements:

1	2	3	4	5	I picked this model to restore because of its historical significance.
1	2	3	4	5	This is the car I dreamed of owning as a kid/young adult.
1	2	3	4	5	I plan to show the car at concourse as well as restoration club meets.
1	2	3	4	5	I plan to trailer the car to the show events I attend.
1	2	3	4	5	I plan on driving the car on weekends, weather permitting.
1	2	3	4	5	I do not plan on driving the car on a regular basis.
1	2	3	4	5	This car is an investment that I need to appreciate in value.
1	2	3	4	5	This car is not just a fun toy that I plan to enjoy.
1	2	3	4	5	Restoring this car helps me make a contribution to society.
1	2	3	4	5	I will be preserving a piece of our culture.
1	2	3	4	5	I would like my children/grandchildren to remember me through this car.
1	2	3	4	5	I am not interested in vintage racing with this car.
1	2	3	4	5	I enjoy learning, reading, and researching cars and parts.
1	2	3	4	5	Money is no object. I want the best car I can find.
1	2	3	4	5	I have the time to tinker with this car.
1	2	3	4	5	The fun is in rebuilding the car not driving it.
1	2	3	4	5	I want people to turn their heads when they see this car.
1	2	3	4	5	No one will know I have a vintage car in my garage.
1	2	3	4	5	I believe cars are modern art.
1	2	3	4	5	Restoring this car is my chance to preserve a part of history.

There are two ways to evaluate your answers. First add the total score from the twenty questions. If the total number is closer to 100, your restoration objective should be focused more on the historically accurate end of the spectrum. If your score is closer to 20, your objective should be to improve the car as a driveable example. An average score is 73, which means most car restoration buffs are more interested in historical accuracy than driveability.

The second way to use this questionnaire is to think about the ideas presented in the questions and write your own purpose statement below.

_____

_____

_____

_____

_____

_____

_____

_____

_____

_____

_____

_____

Evaluation Worksheet for Potential Cars

The Frame (the most important element/should count 40% of the value you place on a car as a potential restoration candidate.)

Look closely to see how badly it is rusted. All frames have some rust. The key is to make sure the rust is not too deep. (The rear cross member usually shows the most rust. Check this area carefully.)

- A badly rusted frame will weaken the car's foundation and cause the body to shift over time.

- Repairing a frame is one of the most costly and difficult repairs to make on any car.

The Frame Grade: _____

The Body (time consuming and costly to fix) should count for about 25% of the value you place on the potential car depending upon how readily available body panels are.

Assess damage especially in the cowl area. Some body damage is easy to fix, but that to the dash wall and trunk wall areas is very difficult.

- Damage to the nose area or fenders is easier to fix.

- Watch out for damage to rear fenders. Replacement parts may not meet original factory specifications as rear damage is less prevalent, and, therefore, fewer parts are available.

The Body Grade: _____

Drive Train (Engine/Transmission/ Rear End should count about 15%)

If you can find a car with its original motor, transmission, and rear end, you will save money and time by not having to track down current replacements.

- With early cars, it is very difficult to know if motors, etc. are original. You can tell if they are correct.

- Don't worry about condition because you will have them rebuilt as part of the restoration.

The Drive Train Grade: _____

Difficult to Replace Parts:

- Stainless window/windshield frames

- Dash/Instruments/Gauges

- Bumpers (expensive to replace/ easy to replate)

- Radio/Special Gadgets (more than $500 for Wonderbar)

- Little knobs and buttons can be time consuming

- Correct Generator, Regulator, Wiper Motor

Difficult to Replace Grade: _____

Usually Easy to Find Parts:

(Easy to find good reproductions, just takes time)

The seat frames and some hardware might be difficult to replace.

- Don't worry about fabric or vinyl areas. They are easy to repair/ replace.

- Convertible Top, Brakes, Vinyl Interiors, Tires, Radiator

Easy to Replace Grade: _____

Example Parts List

Category/Part Description	Actual Cost for 1959 Corvette	Projected Cost for Your Car
Body Repair		
body mount kit	$65	
body panels - new fiberglass	$705	
body panels - used fiberglass	$275	
cowl vent	$14	
splash shield and weather strip	$81	
weather strips - doors, hood, trunk	$81	
sub-total Body Repair	$1,221	
Paint and Preparation		
paint - feather fill, primer, color coat	$700	
sandpaper and vette bond	$100	
sub-total Painting	$800	
Drivetrain Components		
accelerator arm and springs	$31	
air cleaner housing and element	$175	
bell housing and bracket	$192	
carburetors/intake manifold - dual quad	$2,100	
clutch, shield, boot and springs	$56	
crankshaft and rods	$150	
cylinder heads	$375	
distributor - correctly dated	$200	
fan shroud - complete	$175	
fly wheel, pulleys, fan	$300	
generator and adjustment bracket	$218	
horn relay	$25	
ignition shield - carburated type	$283	
oil dipstick, tube and filler cap	$44	
oil pan	$120	
radiator and cap	$331	
shift linkage	$69	
valve covers	$150	
voltage regulator - incorrect, undated	$36	
sub-total Drivetrain Components	$5,030	

Category/Part Description	Actual Cost for 1959 Corvette	Projected Cost for Your Car
Engine Rebuild		
battery cable	$46	_____
camshaft - Duntor hi lift	$167	_____
carburetor rebuild kit	$40	_____
clutch pressure plate and bearing	$175	_____
engine rebuild kit	$264	_____
exhaust manifolds - new	$140	_____
fan belt - undated	$9	_____
fresh air hose and screen	$20	_____
fuel pump - rebuilt	$90	_____
lifters - 16	$73	_____
oil filter	$4	_____
radiator hoses	$41	_____
spark plugs and wires	$84	_____
starter solenoid	$36	_____
valves, springs, guides and seats	$185	_____
water pump - rebuilt	$60	_____
sub-total Engine Rebuild	**$1,434**	
Chassis Overhaul		
battery - tar top	$129	_____
battery tray	$76	_____
brake cylinders, shoes and hoses	$141	_____
brake drums - turned	$32	_____
brake lines	$130	_____
exhaust system	$298	_____
firewall and body grommet set	$45	_____
firewall insulation	$109	_____
fuel lines	$97	_____
master cylinder - rebuilt	$75	_____
suspension kit	$100	_____
tires - 5 new correct	$490	_____
wheel rims and hub caps	$550	_____
sub-total Chassis	**$2,272**	

Category/Part Description	Actual Cost for 1959 Corvette	Projected Cost for Your Car
Operational Mechanical		
antenna lead	$22	_____
ballast resistor	$15	_____
defrost box with hose	$85	_____
fresh air hose and bracket	$33	_____
headlight bulbs and other bulbs	$110	_____
heater hose	$25	_____
hood lock and hinges	$105	_____
road draft tube	$55	_____
speedometer cable	$22	_____
trunk jack, jack handle, wrench - new	$255	_____
trunk liner and mat	$93	_____
trunk tire board kit	$40	_____
wiper arm spacers	$29	_____
wiper motor	$150	_____
sub-total Operations	**$1,039**	

Category/Part Description	Actual Cost for 1959 Corvette	Projected Cost for Your Car
Instrument Panel		
cigarette lighter	$24	_____
clock	$150	_____
dash pad and grab bar vinyl	$231	_____
dash indicator backlight	$22	_____
pedals - gas, brake, clutch	$33	_____
grab bar chrome ends	$46	_____
headlight switch knob and nut	$20	_____
heat, defrost, and air inlet knobs	$27	_____
heater blower switch and cable	$150	_____
horn botton	$26	_____
ignition switch nut and ferule	$19	_____
ignition wiring harness	$59	_____
instrument lenses	$54	_____
main wiring harness	$295	_____
radio and ground strap - Wonderbar	$328	_____
radio speaker and grill	$62	_____
regulator wires	$20	_____
shift boot and pattern	$29	_____
speedometer face and chrome bezel	$55	_____
speedometer rebuild kit	$62	_____
tachometer - high horsepower	$350	_____
temperature control knob	$45	_____
turn signal lever	$10	_____
wiper knob and switch nut	$22	_____
sub-total Instruments	**$2,139**	

Category/Part Description	Actual Cost for 1959 Corvette	Projected Cost for Your Car
Exterior Body		
antenna assembly	$92	_____
bumper mount kit	$44	_____
chrome plating - bumpers, grill, etc.	$2,100	_____
decals - motor, gas, interior	$34	_____
door handles, end caps and kit	$88	_____
door, trunk and ignition lock set	$140	_____
emblems and chrome bezels	$142	_____
headlight assembly and rings	$111	_____
kick panel molding	$30	_____
license plate brackets and seals	$51	_____
outside left hand mirror	$60	_____
park lamp kit	$153	_____
rear reflector kit	$46	_____
side cove moldings, flags and mount kit	$226	_____
soft top latches front and rear	$335	_____
tail lamp lenses	$45	_____
top fender moldings	$180	_____
window felt	$134	_____
windshield and set kit - dated	$384	_____
wiper arms and blades	$75	_____
sub-total Exterior	**$4,470**	

Category/Part Description	Actual Cost for 1959 Corvette	Projected Cost for Your Car
Interior		
ashtray	$23	_____
carpet - daytona red	$175	_____
convertible top and storage felt - dated	$175	_____
dash console plate and insert	$87	_____
door panels w/kickplate and armrest	$634	_____
door window crank handles/lock knobs	$80	_____
lower console molding	$35	_____
package tray and trim	$74	_____
seat belts	$109	_____
seat frame - left bottom	$250	_____
seat vinyl and rebuild padding	$266	_____
shifter, handle, and knob	$403	_____
sill plates - long and step	$197	_____
visors and hardware	$36	
sub-total Interior	**$2,544**	

Grand Total - $20,949

About the author

Paul Iaffaldano is an avid car collector and historian who brings a business insight and perspective to his hobby. He has been the subject of a *Reader's Digest* interview, and his writings have been published in Disney's *Family Fun*. His restoration writing first appeared in *Corvette Trader and Chevy's* Magazine.

Mr. Iaffaldano's writing has a unique flare that comes from his belief that any of life's work should start with a clear objective in mind. "It is not enough to do, we must accomplish." His method of car restoration requires more up-front planning, but ultimately produces a result with longer lasting substance.

He was awarded his Masters of Business degree by Loyola University, Chicago, Illinois, and earned his Bachelors of Arts degree at Wittenberg University, Springfield, Ohio.

MADD

The publisher has pledged to send a portion of the profits of this book to the Mothers Against Drunk Driving organization.